T0024310

# THE LITTLE BOOK OF COTTAGECORE

## TRADITIONAL SKILLS FOR A SIMPLER LIFE

## EMILY KENT

Adams Media
New York London Toronto Sydney New Delhi

Adams Media
An Imprint of Simon & Schuster, Inc.
100 Technology Center Drive
Stoughton, MA 02072

First Adams Media hardcover edition January 2021

ADAMS MEDIA and colophon are trademarks of Simon & Schuster.

For information about special discounts for bulk purchases, please contact Simon & Schuster Special Sales at 1-866-506-1949 or business@simonandschuster.com.

The Simon & Schuster Speakers Bureau can bring authors to your live event. For more information or to book an event contact the Simon & Schuster Speakers Bureau at 1-866-248-3049 or visit our website at www.simonspeakers.com.

Interior design by Stephanie Hannus and Frank Rivera
Interior illustrations by Kathie Kelleher

Manufactured in the United States of America

6  2022

Library of Congress Cataloging-in-Publication Data
Names: Kent, Emily, author.
Title: The little book of cottagecore / Emily Kent.
Description: Avon, Massachusetts: Adams Media, 2021. | Includes index.
Identifiers: LCCN 2020035026 | ISBN 9781507214633 (hc) | ISBN 9781507214640 (ebook)
Subjects: LCSH: Home economics.
Classification: LCC TX145 .K426 2021 | DDC 640--dc23
LC record available at https://lccn.loc.gov/2020035026

ISBN 978-1-5072-1463-3
ISBN 978-1-5072-1464-0 (ebook)

Contains material adapted from the following titles published by Adams Media, an Imprint of Simon & Schuster, Inc.: *The Modern-Day Pioneer* by Charlotte Denholtz, copyright © 2012, ISBN 978-1-4405-5179-6; *The Everything® Small-Space Gardening Book* by Catherine Abbott, copyright © 2012, ISBN 978-1-4405-3060-9; *The Everything® Healthy Tea Book* by Babette Donaldson, copyright © 2014, ISBN 978-1-4405-7459-7; *The Everything® Sewing Book* by Sandra Detrixhe, copyright © 2004, ISBN 978-1-59337-052-7; *The Everything® Pie Cookbook* by Kelly Jaggers, copyright © 2011, ISBN 978-1-4405-2726-5; *The Everything® Cookies & Brownies Cookbook* by Marye Audet, copyright © 2009, ISBN 978-1-60550-125-3.

# CONTENTS

# INTRODUCTION

*Going to your garden to pick your own fruits and vegetables.*
*Filling your kitchen with the aroma of freshly baked bread.*
*Curling up under a quilt you crafted yourself.*

If you've ever yearned for an idyllic life in the country, then cottagecore is for you.

Cottagecore is a movement centered around the simple existence of pastoral life. It focuses on unplugging from the stresses of modern life and instead embracing the wholesomeness and authenticity of nature. It's about experiencing the wistful and the whimsical, doing things that make you feel happy, and living a life of calm relaxation instead of an anxiety-ridden one.

*The Little Book of Cottagecore* will help you make this tranquil way of living a reality regardless of where you live. From container gardening and baking breads from scratch to sewing and cross-stitching and making your own candles and soap, this book is filled with fun hands-on activities that help you unplug from modern life and find solace in the simple things.

Inside you'll find ideas on:

- The easiest plants and herbs for container gardening
- How to bake picture-perfect breads and pies—and the recipes to help!
- Brewing an impeccable cup of tea
- Making your own simple herbal remedies for a variety of ailments
- Crafting unique candles for yourself (or as homemade gifts for others!)
- The ins and outs of making curtains and quilts for your home
- Safely making your own soap

Filled with step-by-step instructions and recipes, this accessible guide will lead you through all the ways you can get back to basics, find calm and comfort, and start living simply and joyfully.

# CHAPTER 1

# GARDENING AND BEEKEEPING

Cottagecore is all about nature and there is no better way to experience the wonders of nature than by growing your own fruits and vegetables. Whether you have a garden of your own, space in a community garden, or space on your patio or balcony, anyone can experience the joys of gardening. This chapter will take you through the best ways to garden in containers and small spaces, but the material can also translate to people who are lucky enough to have a large patch of earth to use as a garden. No matter where you live, you can experience the joys of planting and harvesting your own crops. In addition, this chapter will go over some basic beekeeping skills. Though it is a labor-intensive hobby, there is something so rewarding about gathering your own pure, natural honey for use in both cooking and crafting.

# Container Gardening

If you live in an urban area and the only outdoor space you have is a balcony or porch, growing your vegetables in containers is a great solution. When space is tight, it's best to concentrate on growing small quantities of several different crops and choosing smaller or dwarf varieties of larger plants. Planting in pots is probably the easiest and most common way to grow food on a balcony or patio.

When planning your space, looking at how much sun the area gets is the first step. Most vegetables, herbs, and fruit or berry bushes need at least 6 hours of sunlight each day, so take the time to check this out. If you get less than 6 hours, there are fewer options, but you can still grow many of the vegetables listed in this chapter, such as lettuce or Swiss chard. You should also consider what is the proper-sized container in which to grow your plants. You want to give your plants enough space so they can grow to maturity. Most herb and vegetable plants need a pot with a depth of at least 1 foot of soil to grow their best.

## FINDING CONTAINERS

Containers can be purchased at your local nursery or hardware store. The most common kinds are traditional oak barrels, pots made from reconstituted paper, terra cotta, ceramic, wood, plastic, and resin. If you're planning to grow your vegetables in a container for several years, choose a good-quality one that will last. Containers need to be cleaned on a regular basis to keep them looking good as well as pest- and disease-free, so choose a container you can take care of easily.

To save money, you can recycle items that are no longer fulfilling their original purpose. For example, if growing lettuce, small containers such as milk cartons, a bucket, or an old cooking pot are all wonderful options. When you purchase garden pots, there are usually holes in the bottom of them already. If you're recycling a container, make sure you create at least one good drainage hole so excess water can drain easily.

If you want to grow root crops (such as potatoes and carrots) or beans and peas, you'll need a larger container. Some good choices include Styrofoam coolers, wooden crates, plastic crates (which may need a liner such as landscape fabric in order to hold the soil), and plastic ice cream buckets (ask your local ice cream parlor for their empties). Garbage cans, wooden barrels, metal washbasins, old wheelbarrows that have become rusty and full of holes, or plastic clothes hampers are great options for planting larger crops such as tomatoes, potatoes, and squash.

## PLANTING IN A CONTAINER

Here are eight easy steps for planting in your containers.

1. Select an appropriate-sized container for the plants you are growing that has drainage holes.
2. Fill the container with potting soil to within an inch of the top of the container.
3. Moisten the soil and let it absorb the water before planting (lukewarm water will be absorbed faster than cold water).

4. You can grow several plants in the same pot (except very large ones like tomatoes or squash) and they can be crowded in a bit (about ten small plants will fit in an 18" pot).
5. Set taller plants in the center of the pot and insert stakes prior to planting any other plants around the larger one. If you'll be trellising plants, the larger ones can be placed at the back of the container so they'll climb on the trellis and others can be planted in front.
6. Water once the plants are in the soil; this will help settle the soil and get the roots established quickly.
7. Add more soil, if needed, after watering.
8. Keep the soil moist and well fertilized.

## What Grows Well in a Container

The following are suitable vegetables to grow in containers:

- Beans
- Beets
- Broccoli
- Carrots
- Cucumbers
- Lettuce
- Peas
- Peppers
- Radishes
- Spinach
- Tomatoes

To grow lettuce, spinach, salad greens, radishes, and green onions, you need a container approximately 8"–10" wide and at least 6" deep. In this size container you could grow two or three of your leafy greens and up to a dozen radishes or green onions. For growing carrots, beets, peas, and beans—just remember peas and beans will produce a better harvest if they're grown on a trellis or supported in some way—the best container size is approximately 12"–16" wide and at least 10" deep. If you choose a rectangular container, you could make great use of the space by growing your peas and beans in the back and planting your root crops in front.

Larger vegetables such as tomatoes, cucumbers, cabbage, broccoli, peppers, potatoes, and dwarf corn need a container at least 16" wide with at least 18" of soil to grow well. For best results, use transplants when growing these vegetables (except for potatoes and corn) and grow only one of these plants in each container. To fill up the pot and make it look more attractive, plant lettuce or herbs around the base of the larger plant.

*If you want to grow a lot of vegetables on your balcony or patio, emphasize your vertical space by using trellises or fences. Grow vegetables that can be trained to grow upright, such as snow peas, shelling peas, pole beans, cucumbers, and tomatoes. Choose attractive materials like bamboo, metal, or wood to make trellises or stakes for your plants.*

There are also fruits that do well in containers:

- Blueberries
- Raspberries
- Kumquats
- Lemons
- Dwarf varieties of other fruit trees (must be grown in large pots in the summer and brought indoors or sheltered when the weather gets cold)

Don't solely use potting soil for your fruit trees and shrubs since there is not enough organic matter in it for the plants' needs. Compost is best, or a mix of compost and topsoil. For peaches, nectarines, apricots, and cherries, reduce the topsoil by one quarter and add sand. Once the tree is planted, mulch the top of the container with wood chips to help conserve moisture. Give potted fruit trees and shrubs a thorough watering whenever the top inch of soil feels dry. A little fertilizer (an inch or so of compost or fish fertilizer) should be applied every spring when blossoms start to form. Most fruit trees or shrubs grown in containers will need to be brought indoors or at least protected from the colder winter weather.

## Window Boxes

Even without a balcony or patio to set some pots on, most people have a sunny windowsill that may work just as well. The best option is to hang the box outside a window that opens; the plants will get more natural light and you can easily reach it to water and fertilize the plants.

Most window boxes are approximately 2'–3' in length and 6"–8" deep, although there are many different sizes to choose from. If you don't have a sturdy window ledge to support the box, a lightweight option is probably best. There are some great hooks and hangers for supporting a window box over a balcony railing or on a windowsill. A window box isn't usually very large, so options are more limited, but you can still grow some of your own food.

Some plants that grow well in a window box that doesn't get a lot of heat include:

- Lettuce
- Swiss chard
- Spinach

If your window box gets a great deal of sun, these plants would be a better option:

- Parsley
- Chives
- Basil
- Peas
- Beans (if they can be trellised in some way)

When planting your window box, choose plants that will work best for your location. If the area isn't too hot, lettuce or spinach will grow in a shallow window box. However, if the area gets a lot of heat, some annual herbs such as basil, parsley, and chives could be a better option for you.

 *Containers, bagged gardens, and window boxes will need watering every day, especially if the area gets full sun, so check your planters regularly. Have a hose stored under your sink so you have easy access for watering your balcony or patio garden.*

Many herbs can be grown indoors in pots during the winter months. Place them in proper-sized containers and position them near a sunny window so you can enjoy using them all winter long. Grow perennials such as marjoram, chives, mint, and winter savory from divisions or cuttings taken in the fall. Basil, dill, and parsley are annuals and will need to be started from seed outdoors (in pots) in late summer then transplanted to larger pots in the fall. When growing herbs indoors, make sure you use a light, well-draining potting soil and water as needed. Try not to overwater the plants or let them dry out.

## Bagged Garden

Another option is growing your herbs and vegetables in a bagged garden. You can get a shallow plastic container and place the bag of potting mix or a burlap sack into it. Make sure you poke a few drainage holes in the bag, then turn it over and cut a flap in the top of the bag to expose the soil for planting. The plastic container will hold moisture as well as keep the area clean—it will act the same as a tray under a container—just make sure there's no water sitting in the plastic container since most plants don't like their roots to be too wet as they can start to rot.

A bagged garden is an excellent option for growing:

- Tomatoes
- Potatoes
- Carrots
- Beets
- Cabbage

## Fruit Growing Basics

Most fruits are put into two categories: small fruits and tree fruits. Among the small fruits are strawberries, raspberries, blueberries, currants, blackberries, and gooseberries. Small fruits usually grow on either bushes or canes, except for strawberries which are a low-growing bedding plant.

Bushes have permanent spreading branches that grow to about 4' high and just as wide. Blueberries and currants grow on bushes. If you have a small space, these can be trained to grow as espalier along a fence or wall.

Canes are slender shrubs that have stems starting at ground level. They need to be controlled by being trained along a stake and wire or string and they need to be cut back each year after fruiting so there's room for new growth. Raspberries and blackberries grow on canes.

## POLLINATION

Most flowers need to be pollinated to develop into fruit. Pollen is usually transferred from one plant to another by the wind or insects. Small fruits, except for blueberries, can be fertilized by their own plant.

## BERRY PATCH

Berries are easy to grow so long as they get enough sunlight and moisture. To ensure a good crop, separate the older fruit-bearing canes from the new by tying the new growth together or tagging it so you can easily identify what's old and new. Once the fruit has finished on the older stalks they can be cut back. This provides room for new growth and allows light to reach it.

Berries such as blueberries or blackberries can be grown successfully against a wall or fence to maximize your small space.

### Blackberries

Blackberries can be grown either erect or trailing.

- **Botanical name:** *Rubus fruticosus*
- **Family name:** Rosaceae
- **Growing characteristics:** Best grown in a sunny location but will take partial shade.
- **Soil:** Well-drained soil with a pH of about 5.5 is best.

- **Water and fertilizer:** Require adequate moisture all season. A month or so before new growth starts in the spring, apply 10–10–10 fertilizer (½ pound per 10' row).
- **When to plant:** Canes are best planted in early fall. If the ground doesn't freeze plant them up until early spring.
- **Care:** Disease and insects are kept at bay by planting your bush in an area that's been cultivated for several years. Choose disease-resistant varieties. Remove old canes after harvest and keep plants free of weeds and fallen leaves.
- **Harvest:** Berries start producing in August.

## Blueberries

Check with your local nursery for the best varieties to grow in your area.

- **Botanical name:** *Vaccinium corymbosum*
- **Family name:** Ericaceae
- **Growing characteristics:** Blueberries do best in a sunny location but will grow in partial shade.
- **Soil:** They need an acidic soil with a pH of 5.0–6.0; if you have an alkaline soil, plant your blueberries in pots. Blueberries are not completely self-fertile, so plant two varieties together to ensure good pollination.
- **Water and fertilizer:** Like water-retentive soil. In the spring, apply a high-nitrogen fertilizer (½–1 ounce per square yard). If you have sandy soil, do a second application a month later.
- **When to plant:** Plant in the fall or spring 3'–4' apart.

- **Care:** In northern climates, bushes should be protected from the cold winds. In summer, mulch your plants with well-rotted manure, compost, or peat. You may need to use netting to protect your bushes from birds.
- **Harvest:** June or July.

### Currants and Gooseberries

Currants and gooseberries can be grown in most areas. Red currants do best in cooler, humid regions. Black currants are not as popular.

- **Botanical name:** *Ribes*
- **Family name:** Rosaceae
- **Growing characteristics:** Currants and gooseberries grow on a bush. They grow well in either a sunny location or in partial shade. They flower early in the year, so choose an area that will be less likely to get a heavy frost.
- **Soil:** They like water-retaining but well-drained soil.
- **Water and fertilizer:** Water only during prolonged dry spells and fertilize in late winter or early spring. Use a complete fertilizer and place around the base of the bush.
- **When to plant:** Plant in early spring or in the fall.
- **Care:** Take out any suckers that grow from the main stem or the roots. Control weeds by mulching. Birds are a common problem and placing netting over your bushes will help.
- **Harvest:** Pick when fully ripe.

Raspberries

The best way to grow raspberries is in a row with the canes trained between stakes and wires.

- **Botanical name:** *Rubus idaeus*
- **Family name:** Rosaceae
- **Growing characteristics:** Raspberries generally do best in full sun but can be grown in partial shade.
- **Soil:** They like a soil that is slightly acidic and well drained but with moisture retention. Raspberries don't do well on slopes, especially if the soil drains quickly. Try placing them where they'll have some protection from wind or cold. Canes that have produced fruit die and are replaced every year by new canes that grow from the roots.
- **Water and fertilizer:** Water well in warm or dry spells. Mulch with manure, compost, or peat to help retain moisture. Apply horse manure in the fall and fertilize approximately one month before growth starts in the spring.
- **When to plant:** Plant one-year-old canes in the fall.
- **Care:** Keep well weeded; hand weeding is best as hoeing between the canes can damage the shallow root system. Canes need to be supported and you can do this by placing posts at either end of your row and stringing wire between them on either side of the canes.
- **Harvest:** Some varieties bear fruit midsummer on the previous season's shoots; others fruit in early or mid-fall on the current growth.

## Strawberries

There are two different kinds of strawberries. One produces only one crop of fruit and the other is an ever-bearing kind that produces one crop in early summer and another in mid-fall. Ever-bearing strawberries are usually less hardy and don't store fresh for long.

- **Botanical name:** *Fragaria*
- **Family name:** Rosaceae
- **Growing characteristics:** Strawberries like sunny locations.
- **Soil:** They like fertile, well-drained soil that is slightly acidic with a pH of 5.5–6. The soil should have enough organic matter that it will retain moisture.
- **Water and fertilizer:** Water regularly in dry weather, especially when ripening begins, and during the first few weeks after planting new plants. Apply a complete fertilizer in late winter.
- **When to plant:** Plant in either spring or fall. Ever-bearing varieties are best planted in the spring.
- **Care:** In the first season, remove the blooms from one-crop varieties that were planted in the fall or spring. On ever-bearing varieties, remove flowers in early spring to encourage more and better berries later in the season. Runners will freely grow once the plants are actively growing and these can be cut off to make sure more energy goes to producing more fruit. A three-year cycle is the usual method for strawberries. Young plants are set out in the spring for harvesting the next summer. The next year,

these plants will produce less and should be removed right after fruiting. To get a bumper crop of strawberries, you want to set out new plants each year. Once berries start to form, tuck dry straw under the berries to keep them from touching the ground (this makes them less susceptible to rotting). In the fall, cut off any runners that have grown (this conserves the plant's energy). Control weeds with shallow hoeing.

- **Harvest:** To ensure good flavor, pick strawberries with their stems attached when the berries are fully ripened all around. They bruise easily so avoid excessive handling.

## Growing Herbs

In almost every culture in history, there are references to using herbs for preparing and preserving food, scenting the air, and treating illnesses and wounds. Most herbs are wild, tough plants that haven't changed despite being cultivated for centuries.

When planning your herb garden, first decide where you'd like to locate the plants. If you're keeping your herbs outside, consider growing them near the back or front door so the plants will be easily accessible from the kitchen.

When harvesting herbs, be sure to pick them early in the morning. The best time is just after the dew has dried but before the sun has hit the leaves. The reason for this is the essential oils found in the herb leaves lose their quality of flavor and fragrance once the leaves are exposed to heat.

When harvesting perennial herbs such as thyme, mint, and lavender, it's important not to harvest too much of the plant in the first year of growth; if the plant is cut back too much, the root system will not be able to develop properly. A light trim will help shape the plant and encourage bushiness. Once the plant has become established, you can harvest up to two-thirds of the plant each season.

Most annual and biennial plants can be cut several times over the season, and a good rule of thumb is to cut the top half of the plant at each cutting. Just before the first frost, either pull the plant or cut it at ground level. The same is true when harvesting biennials such as parsley. If you're growing to save herb seeds, find a way to mark the plant early in the season and don't cut it so it will produce a large amount of seeds. If you're growing the plant in a container, write a note on the pot. If you're planting it in the ground, perhaps place it on the edge of your herb garden. Anything to remind you you're treating that plant differently from the others will do the trick. Biennials will not produce seeds until the second year.

## Beekeeping: A Short Introduction

Bees are an essential part of agriculture, necessary for pollinating plants to ensure better fruits and bigger crops. In this section, you will learn the basics of beekeeping, but know that this is an intense process for only the most dedicated of people.

Before beginning this hobby, make sure you have a thorough understanding of the complexities of keeping bees.

Honeybees can be kept almost anyplace that has flowering plants producing nectar and pollen. Choose a site for beehives that is discreet, sheltered from winds, and partially shaded. Avoid low spots in a yard where cold, damp air accumulates in winter.

## THE HIVE LOCATION

The best beehive location is one where your best source of pollen and nectar is within two square miles of your hive—the closer the better. Because bees use pollen and nectar to produce their own energy, the farther they have to travel for it, the more they have to consume themselves. In contrast, if you place them closer to their food source, you can collect more honey.

 *Before you begin beekeeping, know that most states have very strict laws as to where hives can be placed and who can keep them. You need to understand the laws of your state before you begin.*

Position your hive so the entrance faces east, this way the early morning sun will alert them to the new day. Because flower nectar often evaporates in the morning hours during the summer, the sooner bees are out of their hive foraging, the more honey they are likely to produce. The best position for a hive is where it will also have afternoon shade, shielding the hive from the summer sun. Shade, rather than sunlight, will give the bees more time to concentrate their efforts on making honey since they won't need to work on carrying water back to cool the hive.

## BASIC BEEKEEPING EQUIPMENT

A man-made hive is built to imitate the spaces bees leave between their honeycombs in nature. The dimensions are fairly standard and should be copied exactly if you decide to make your own beehives.

The following equipment is used within a hive:

- **Bottom board:** a wooden stand that the hive rests upon. Bottom boards can be set on bricks, concrete blocks, cinder blocks, or any stable base to keep the hive off the ground.
- **Hive body or brood super:** a large wooden box that holds eight to ten frames of comb. In this space, the bees rear their brood and store honey for their own use. Up to three brood supers can be used for a brood nest.
- **Queen excluder:** a frame made with wire mesh placed between the brood super and the honey super.
- **Honey supers:** shallow boxes with frames of comb hanging in them for bees to store surplus honey.
- **Frames and foundation:** frames hang inside each super or box on a specially cut ledge, called a rabbet. Frames keep the combs organized inside your hive and allow you to easily and safely inspect your bees.
- **Covers:** you'll need an inner and outer cover.

- **Smoker:** this calms bees and reduces stinging; pine straw, sawdust, chipped wood mulch, grass, and burlap make good smoker fuel.
- **Hive tool:** used for prying apart supers and frames.
- **Bee suit or jacket, veil, gloves, ankle protection, and gauntlet:** this is all personal protective gear worn when working with bees.
- **Feeders:** these hold sugar syrup that is fed to the bees in early spring and in fall.

## PURCHASING BEES

Usually the best way to start keeping bees is to buy established colonies from a local beekeeper. Often a local beekeeper might even have a colony he or she wants to give away. It's better to get two colonies at the beginning because that allows you to interchange frames of both brood and honey if one colony becomes weaker than the other and needs a boost. Have the beekeeper open the supers. The bees should be calm and numerous enough that they fill most of the spaces between combs.

Moving a hive is a two-person job and it's easiest to move a hive during winter when they're lighter and populations are low. The first thing to do is close the hive entrance (you can accomplish this with a piece of folded window screen), then look for any cracks and seal them with duct tape. Make sure the supers are fastened together and the bottom board is stapled to the last super. Remember to open the hive entrance after the hive is relocated.

*If you're buying colonies, know that the condition of the equipment usually reflects the care the bees have received. If you find colonies housed in rotting hives, don't purchase them.*

You can also buy packaged bees and queens. Bees are commonly shipped in 2- to 5-pound packages of about 10,000 to 20,000 bees. Keep the packages cool and shaded when they arrive. To transfer bees to their new hive, set up a bottom board with one hive body and remove half of the frames. Spray the bees heavily with sugar syrup (one part sugar to one part water) through the screen on the package; the bees will gorge themselves with syrup and become sticky, making them easy to pour.

The next step is to move the queen, which will be in a separate cage. Pry off the package's lid, remove the can of syrup provided for transit, find and remove the queen cage, and reclose the package. The queen cage has holes at both ends plugged with cork. Under the cork at one end you'll see it's filled with white "queen candy." Remove the cork from this end and suspend the queen cage between two center frames in your hive. Worker bees will eventually eat through the candy and release the queen.

Shake the original package lightly to move all the bees into a pile at the bottom. Take the lid off the package again and pour the bees into the hive on top of the queen. As they slowly spread throughout the hive, carefully return the frames to their original positions and replace the inner and outer covers of the hive. Be sure to feed the bees sugar water until natural nectar starts to appear.

## BEEKEEPING THROUGHOUT THE YEAR

You want your bees to be at their maximum strength before the nectar flow begins, that way the created honey is stored for harvest rather than used to build up their strength. Feeding and medicating your bees should be done in January through February. Because the queens resume egg laying in January, some colonies will need supplemental feedings of sugar syrup.

By mid-February, you should inspect your hives for population growth, the arrangement of the brood nest, and disease symptoms. If one of your colonies has less brood than average, you can strengthen it by transferring a frame of sealed brood from your other colony.

If you use two brood supers and find that most of the bees and brood are in the upper super, reverse the supers, placing the top one on the bottom. You want to do this because it relieves congestion. When a colony feels congested, it swarms, looking for another place to live. If you only have one brood super, you'll need to relieve congestion by providing additional honey supers above a queen excluder.

Annual requeening can be done in early spring or in the fall. Most feel that requeening is one of the best investments a beekeeper can make. Young queens not only lay eggs more prolifically, they also secrete higher levels of pheromones, which stimulate the worker bees to forage.

In order to requeen a colony, you must find, kill, and discard the old queen, then allow the colony to remain queen-less for 24 hours. Once that time has passed, you can introduce the new queen in her cage, allowing the workers to eat through the candy in order to release her.

By mid-April, your colonies should be strong enough to collect surplus nectar. This is when you should add honey supers above the hive bodies. Add enough supers to accommodate both the incoming nectar and the large bee population. Adding supers stimulates foraging and limits late season swarming.

During late summer and early autumn, brood and honey production drops. At this point, you should crowd the bees by giving them only one or two honey supers. This forces bees to store honey in the brood nest to strengthen the hive. Colonies usually overwinter in two hive bodies or one hive body and at least one honey super. Make sure that if you overwinter in one hive body and a honey super, you remove the queen excluder so the queen can move up into the honey super during winter. If your colony is light on stores, feed them heavy syrup (two parts sugar to one part water). Bees should have between 50 to 60 pounds of stores going into winter. A hive with a full deep frame weighs 6 pounds and a full shallow frame weighs 3 pounds. (You can pick up the frame to estimate the weight of the hive and stores.) Never allow stores to drop below 12 to 18 pounds.

## Gathering Honey

It's best to harvest your honey on a sunny, windless day, since bees are calmest then. Remove the bees from the hive by blowing smoke into the hive opening. After a few minutes, pry the outer cover loose and lift it off. Blow more smoke through the hole in the inner cover, then remove it. Once the inner cover is removed, again blow smoke into the hive to drive the bees downward and out of the way. Remove the super and pry the frames loose with the hive tool. Be careful not to crush any bees; a crushed bee releases a scent that stimulates other bees to attack. Gently brush off any bees clinging to the frames. A comb that's ready to be harvested should be about 80 percent sealed over.

Uncap the combs in a bee-proof location, like a tightly screened room, as bees will want to take the honey if they can get to it. Slice off the comb tops with a sharp knife warmed in hot water. (A heavy kitchen knife is fine.) It's best to use two knives, cutting with one while the other is warming. Once the honey is extracted, return the emptied combs to the hive for the bees to clean and use again. With care, combs can be recycled for twenty years or more.

If you do keep bees, remember that you can use your honeycombs to obtain wax for your candle making in Chapter 5.

# CHAPTER 2

# TEA TIME

B rewing a healthy cup of tea is pleasurable, simple, and economical. All you need is some fresh tea that's been stored well, a cup, and good-quality water. Of these three, water is the most critical component. Certainly there are differences in the amount of antioxidants, polyphenols, tannins, and thearubigins in the tea, but the simple fact that water constitutes 99 percent of a cup of brewed tea makes it far and away the most important contributor to the health of what you drink as well as the flavor you'll enjoy.

The techniques with which tea is brewed and the equipment used—an elegant tea set, formal ceremonial tools, or a simple mug—also create ambience and may enhance the pleasure of the moment. And don't forget that creating a bit of beauty and sharing pleasurable moments with friends and family can be very healing. Learning some of the tried-and-true techniques of healthy tea brewing will certainly expand the possibilities of what tea drinking can be.

## Beyond the Basics

Tea can be exorbitantly expensive and so complex that it prompts a lifetime of study. Some techniques for brewing fine tea consist of several steps. In addition to the amount of tea, temperature of the water, and choice of cup, other "rules" for preparation can involve the way in which the tea is placed in the brewing vessel, how the teapot is prepared, the way the water is poured over the tea, the placement of the brewing tools, hand positions during the process, and many others. Attention to these details is not always restricted to ceremonies. For some tea lovers, it's a matter of style. Tea aficionados incorporate some of these disciplines into their personal style to precisely control and maximize the experience. Examples include brewing the leaves in a pre-warmed teapot versus a cold teapot in order to hold the water at a more even temperature; swirling the water to stir the leaves in the pot so the leaves' surfaces are all equally moistened; and knowing that hand position on a teapot or gaiwan (a Chinese lidded tea bowl) can be both a gesture of elegance and an efficient way to ensure the tea isn't spilled.

New brewing innovations are introduced to tea lovers every year. Many are designed for convenience, others increase the elegance and delight of the tea experience, but all seek to enhance the experience of the individual who desires to develop a personal taste for tea. Regardless, the basics of brewing remain the same. Perhaps the one great secret to a fine cup is that there are no rules, only the invitation.

## Water: 99 Percent of a Good Cup of Tea

Lu Yu, author of *The Classic of Tea*, considered water to be the mother of tea. Many tea masters teach about the marriage of leaf and water. There's probably not a single tea author or educator who fails to mention the importance of selecting quality water for brewing tea. Many quote Lu Yu's original teaching that fresh spring water is best. Most people don't have a source of fresh spring water but they do have different sources from which to choose. Selecting a favorite water is just like selecting a favorite tea; whether it's filtered tap water or bottled, there is no "best" choice except to satisfy individual tastes.

*The differences in water can be demonstrated by conducting a water tasting. Select several different water sources, such as fresh tap water, two-day-old tap water, boiled tap water that has cooled, filtered tap water, and a few different brands of unflavored bottled water. Pour the same amount into identical glasses. Compare their smells, appearances, and flavors. Have an assistant number the glasses and switch the order so your tasting will be "blind." Then, using the same tea for each, brew a cup with each type of water and compare.*

Donna Fellman and Lhasha Tizer tell one of the most unique stories about brewing tea with special water in their book *Tea Here*

*Now*. They describe a Vietnamese tradition in which lotus flowers are filled with tea leaves just before they close at sunset. The next morning, just before dawn, dew is collected from the lotus leaves as soon as the flowers open and used to brew lotus-scented tea.

## THE FLAVOR OF WATER

Water that has a pleasing flavor and feel in the mouth is usually good for tea. Fresher water is also preferred because it has more oxygen in it, and for this reason many tea drinkers use filtered tap water. However, many municipal water districts add chemicals like fluoride and chlorine to their water supply in concentrations that some people can taste. Plumbing in older homes can add unpleasant flavors and even minerals and rust to water. Private wells draw minerals from the ground water. In most instances, a good filter can eliminate these issues and greatly improve the flavor of the water.

Bottled water provides an option for those with poor-quality tap water, but there are some cautions there as well. Some bottled water is highly mineralized while others can leave a slightly oily sensation in the mouth that may affect the flavor of the tea. Other choices, like distilled water, can have a flat taste, which can also detract from a flavorful tea. Lastly, poor-quality plastic can give bottled water an unpleasant taste.

## How to Heat Your Water

The most important "rule" about heating water is to heat it only once. Don't fill a kettle and then boil it multiple times. Heat only what is needed and refill it with fresh water for additional infusions; this way, the water will retain a fresh and bright flavor. Repeatedly boiling water tends to reduce the amount of oxygen present and "flatten" the flavor.

When using whole-leaf tea, it's important for the leaves to have room to float in the water so the hot water touches every surface evenly. Getting to know how a tea will change as it's infused is helpful for choosing a vessel. Whole leaves should have enough room to float in the water with all surfaces exposed.

In his book *The Classic of Tea*, tea sage Lu Yu described the various stages of boiling water: the first, tiny bubbles the size of shrimp or crab eyes, then fish eyes, then the size of pearls, and ultimately the full rolling boil. Each stage has a unique sound. Almost without realizing it, people who consistently use a kettle recognize the rumble of their water gradually coming to a boil and reach for it just before hearing the whistle. Although this isn't as accurate as a beverage thermometer, most tea drinkers instinctively gauge the temperature they want for their tea by the sound of the water approaching full boil. Gaining popularity, electric kettles make brewing tea even easier, although they lack the romance of an old-fashioned whistling teakettle.

## Using Tea Leaves

One of the most delightful moments of using whole over cut leaves is watching them unfurl and return to their original form. Some artisan teas that are bud-only, like Silver Needle, stand vertically when they're brewed. Activated by the hot water, they look a bit like little dancers in the water. Other teas, like Jasmine Pearl, slowly unroll. Using a glass teapot allows tea brewers and guests to watch, like peeking through a window, and enjoy the entire process.

### HANDLING THE DRY LEAF

It is important to use a clean teaspoon or scoop to transfer the leaves from the bag or your caddy. Because they are extremely hygroscopic (meaning they readily absorb moisture), they also absorb aromas from the air as well as from other surfaces with which they come in contact. Measuring the tea in the palm of your hand risks flavoring it with soap, perfume, or another kitchen aroma if you've been preparing food.

### HOW MUCH TEA?

Most people measure their tea with a teaspoon or tea scoop, but most recommended servings offered by retailers are written in grams. This is because there's such a large difference between the large, flat, fluffy leaves as in a White Peony tea as compared to a tightly rolled green Gunpowder tea. A teaspoonful of each of these kinds of leaves would be very different; there wouldn't be enough of the fluffy leaf and there'd be far too much of the tightly rolled one.

*Compare a brand name tea bag with its loose-leaf equivalent. Using a small digital scale set to measure grams, open a tea bag and weigh the contents. Most tea bags contain 2–3 grams. Set this aside and weigh out an equal amount of the same kind of tea as whole leaf. Compare the visual differences between the two, then brew a cup of each and compare the aroma and flavor.*

Fortunately, once you brew a new tea, the experience will guide the next cup: more or less tea, more or less brewing time, etc. The more experienced you become with various whole-leaf teas, the more instinctive the brewing will become. The accuracy of weighing tea by the gram is essential to the professional tea taster, less so for the amateur tea lover. Considerations like "how much tea" become part of the intimate relationship you develop with the leaf.

## MULTIPLE INFUSIONS

There is an expression for brewing whole-leaf tea with the intention of creating multiple infusions that gradually rehydrate and restore the leaf: the agony of the leaf. With several brief infusions, the leaf gradually unfolds from its twisted or wrapped-up form and the flavors peel off in thin layers like those of an onion. The possible number of infusions may be as few as two or as many as seven, each one still offering an interesting cup. This is a technique that some tea lovers use privately, brewing a batch of tea several times during the day, creating a strong breakfast brew, a moderate midday cup, and a gentle evening tea.

## WASHING THE LEAF

There is a step in brewing whole-leaf tea where the server "washes" the leaves with a quick rinse of warm water—about 30 seconds—and then discards that liquid. There are many interpretations for why this is done. One is that, being an agricultural product, the leaves are rinsed to remove any extraneous dust that may be present. Another possible reason is that, during the time the tea has been shipped, repackaged, and stored, some of the leaves were broken and those small bits are rinsed away. Yet another is that the surface of the leaf is thought not to offer the best flavor. A quick rinse opens the surface cells and reveals the sweeter flavors within. Try it and decide if this is a step you wish to incorporate into your own brewing practice.

## Choosing the Perfect Teapot

Teapots are made from many different materials, in a variety of sizes and shapes. Some of the smallest are designed for serving

Chinese-style tea to a small group while larger ones are generally used for serving Western-style tea to several people. Teapots of all sizes can be made from Yixing clay, fine porcelain, earthenware clay, silver, glass, stainless steel, and cast iron. Select a teapot based on the number of people to be served and your preferred method of brewing. In general, add only the amount of tea and enough water to the pot so, after steeping, there will be no water remaining on the leaves that might become bitter. Many teas, both loose-leaf and bagged, will brew a second flavorful pot, but you may have to allow a longer steeping time for the second infusion.

Teapots tend to develop a patina on the inside with frequent use. This discoloration troubles some, who prefer to wash it away to keep the inside of the teapot as spotless as the outside. Others take pride in the coloration or staining on the inside of the pot as it ages and feel it contributes a bit of flavor to each future use. With this in mind, some tea lovers reserve certain teapots for particular kinds of tea (for example, one for brewing green tea and another for black).

## Tea Balls versus Tea Bags

Two early inventions changed tea drinking for Westerners. One was the infuser called the tea ball or tea egg. The second was the disposable tea bag accidentally invented by Thomas Sullivan, an American tea importer. Both innovations kept tea leaves confined so they could be neatly controlled.

## TEA BALLS

Silversmiths in the late 1800s enjoyed a great demand for fanciful, perforated balls with lids that could be filled with tea leaves, then suspended by a thin chain into a teapot or directly into a teacup. The beauty of these pieces makes them of interest to collectors, even if they aren't used as frequently today. One of the associated problems is that tea leaves expand as they rehydrate, crowding the tea balls, so the tea doesn't infuse as well. A second issue is that the leaves are a little more difficult to clean out of the ball.

## TEA BAGS

The tea bag came a bit later, when American tea entrepreneur Thomas Sullivan sent samples of his teas sewed into small cloth bags as substitutes for more expensive metal tins. His customers didn't understand Sullivan's intention and brewed the tea sample without opening the bag. They were delighted with the convenience of this new innovation and immediately ordered more tea in these handy little bags. Sullivan quickly found a way to produce more bags and is remembered today as the inventor of the tea bag. Tea bags continue to evolve and they are the most popular way to brew tea today. And while most bagged tea is manufactured to brew a full-bodied cup without bitterness at almost any temperature, there are usually suggestions printed on the package.

## COST OF CONVENIENCE

The problem with both tea balls and tea bags is that, as the tea absorbs water, it expands and fills the bag or ball, preventing water from flowing evenly through the leaves to extract the full flavor. To alleviate this problem, tea leaves are now cut into tiny pieces and blended with fine particles of tea called fannings and dust. There are no definitive studies on whether or not the chemical compounds in the leaf are reduced as a result, but it is generally thought to be so. Even though tea bags have improved and most kinds of tea are sold this way, fine-quality teas are not likely to use them.

## Making a Proper British Tea

The round-bellied teapot is usually associated with a "proper" British afternoon tea. Tea bags are often preferred for brewing in teapots because they can be easily removed as soon as the liquid reaches the desired strength and cleanup is simplified. When putting whole-leaf tea directly into the pot, there are two methods for controlling the period of time the leaves are steeped so they can be used for a second infusion: the one-pot method and the two-pot method. With both methods, the amount of tea is the same, usually one tea bag or one teaspoon (or whatever the adjusted amount given the tea) per person, plus one for the pot.

## ONE-POT METHOD

Tea is added to the teapot with just enough water for a first serving for all guests. The tea may be added as loose leaves or contained in an infusion device such as a basket, tea ball, or tea bag. All of the tea is served for the first infusion so excess tea doesn't sit with the leaves, becoming bitter. Freshly boiled water for a second infusion is added when needed. Once again, only the amount of water that will be poured is added to the pot.

## TWO-POT METHOD

A full pot of tea is brewed in one teapot and then decanted into a second teapot for serving. The first teapot with the leaves can be set aside and brewed a second or third time. The advantage is the full teapot can be kept on a votive candle warmer or electric warmer and served over time without additional brewing.

## Brewing Different Types of Tea

It cannot be said often enough that a good cup of tea can only be determined by individual taste. There are guidelines but there are no exact recipes or formulas to be followed that will satisfy all people or tastes. Even the generalization that lighter teas are brewed with cooler water for less time can be limiting and sometimes misleading. This brief overview of tea categories should be considered a starting place, knowing that much of the richness of the tea experience comes from experimentation.

## BREWING GREEN TEA

Most green teas are sensitive to temperature and time, becoming bitter if infused with boiling water or if left in the water for too long. Using water that is cooler than the boiling point works well for most green teas (typically around 180°F). Pour over the leaves only the amount you will use immediately. Steep for 1–2 minutes for the first infusion and about 3–4 minutes for a second.

## BREWING BLACK TEA

Black teas can usually tolerate very hot water, almost to a full boil. In fact, many tea drinkers prefer the bold, bracing brew that comes from an aggressive infusion. Others like to peel away the layers of flavor of multiple infusions by beginning with a very light cup. Darjeeling teas are an example of a black tea that may be better brewed with slightly cooler temperatures and less time. By doing so, these are more likely to offer several good infusions. Most other black teas can also be steeped for longer periods without astringency, for up to 5 minutes, though this reduces the number of times the same leaves can be infused and still provide a pleasant cup.

## BREWING OOLONG TEA

Since oolong tea is more varied and complex as a category, there is not a standard practice for brewing. The range of low oxidation (green) to almost completely oxidized (black) leaves makes this impossible. Recommendations are to use techniques for brewing green and black teas relative to the type of oolong.

For greener oolongs, use lower-temperature water, and for a more fully oxidized leaf, use warmer water.

## BREWING PU'ERH TEA

Like oolong tea, pu'erh is a category with such enormous diversity that simple guidelines are of little value. The darkness of the brewed tea, the intensity of flavor, along with the mellowness provided by actual fermentation (rather than oxidation), mean that a short steeping will still be earthy and rich. On the other hand, some pu'erh teas can be steeped for more than 10 minutes without bitterness. Brewing preferences will also vary between younger and more aged pu'erh. Because the flavor is so different from other teas, newcomers may want to visit a tearoom to sample or join an organized tasting before making their first purchase.

## BREWING WHITE TEA

Instructions for brewing white tea usually compare it with brewing green tea, recommending lower temperatures and a shorter steeping time. This results in a pale liquid with a very subtle flavor. Using near boiling water and steeping for 3 minutes darkens the liquid and intensifies the flavor, releasing some of the definitive creaminess unique to white tea. The lack of astringency and bitterness allows this tea to be brewed many different ways.

## BREWING HERBAL TEA

When preparing bagged herbal teas and functional teas, it is highly recommended to follow the package directions. There are many herb blends where hot water and an extended steeping time are recommended to release the active ingredients. When using combinations of whole herbal products, it may be necessary to infuse some ingredients separately, such as boiling roots longer than steeping leaves, then combining the "teas" in the teapot or cup.

## BREWING FLAVORED TEA

Tea leaves that have been flavored by adding food-grade oils have a tendency to lose flavor more rapidly than natural teas. For this reason, flavored teas do not usually produce very full-bodied second infusions and may also have a shorter shelf life. Since black, green, and white teas are now available with added flavoring essences, the temperature at which they are brewed should be based on the basic category—boiling water for black tea but cooler temperatures for green and white.

## Iced Tea Brewing Basics

The story of iced tea first being served at the India Pavilion of the 1904 World's Fair in St. Louis is often interpreted as the origin of tea being poured over ice. Evidence to the contrary documents that iced tea was served in September of 1890 at a Civil War reenactment in Nevada, Missouri. Local newspapers reported that iced sweet tea had been served for the participants and described the cold tea as a luxury for hot southern summers.

Discussion on the difference between the two stories suggests that Richard Blechynden, the World's Fair tea merchant who was struggling to interest anyone in his tea, borrowed the suggestion to serve it cold and thereby popularized the innovative practice. But even earlier, in the 1820s, cold tea punches were served in the South, blending tea with alcohol. A recipe in *The Kentucky Housewife*, a cookbook by Mrs. Lettice Bryan published in 1839, combines a strong tea with a considerable amount of sugar, sweet cream, and claret that should be served cold.

### BREWING ICED TEA

Any tea can be brewed hot and then chilled and served over ice, but there are some teas that become cloudy when cold and look less appealing when served.

Some tips for brewing iced tea:

- Brew the tea at least twice as strong as you would for hot tea by using a higher ratio of tea to water to make it stronger. Do not steep it for any longer.
- Cool before pouring over ice so the tea does not become too diluted.
- Adding sweetener when the tea is still hot makes it dissolve more rapidly and evenly but assumes that everyone will want sweet tea.

- The best-dissolving sweetener for serving unsweetened iced tea to guests when it's already cold is a sugar syrup. This is thinner than honey or agave nectar and blends with the tea almost instantly.
- A pinch of baking soda (no more than ⅛ teaspoon per gallon) helps neutralize the tannins and reduce bitterness.
- Refrigerating tea can make it turn cloudy. Better to brew only what is needed for the day and keep it at room temperature.
- Adding a sprig of mint or a lemon slice to the glass is both flavorful and decorative.

## Cold Brewing

Cold brewing is a technique that can be used with any kind of tea and is the simplest and possibly healthiest way to brew. Combine your choice of tea and water in a glass container and refrigerate for 8 or more hours. This method works especially well with green and light oolongs (flavors are smoother and sweeter). This does not risk the unhealthy bacteria that can grow in sun-brewed tea.

Taking cold brew a step further, new innovations of infusers suspend a vessel for ice over a small repository of tea under which is the final pitcher to catch the brewed tea. As the ice melts, it soaks the tea, drop by drop. In very slow motion, the leaves are first saturated and then slowly give up their tea, each highly concentrated drop falling into the waiting pitcher.

This is not a brew to be gulped but savored. Each tiny sip is an intense experience. This method is often used with Japanese teas like gyokuro and sencha.

# CHAPTER 3

# BAKING BREADS, PIES, AND COOKIES

O f all the home-centered crafts in the cottagecore lifestyle, baking is one of the most rewarding—after all, you get to eat your delicious creations once you've made them! This chapter will take you through the basics of baking breads, from the proper ingredients and equipment to use to the science behind what's going on in your oven as those fabulous aromas are released. You'll also find a myriad of wholesome recipes for breads, pies, and cookies to try.

## Breadmaking Basics

There aren't many ingredients in bread but everything has a vital importance. Understanding what works and why will help your creative juices flow and assist in troubleshooting if problems arise.

## FLOUR

Flour is the most important ingredient in breadmaking. It provides the structure (or "crumb") of the bread as well as most of its nutritional value. The grain most commonly used is wheat. Although other grains are used, wheat alone contains enough essential gluten proteins to make bread production possible.

### Bread Flour

The most common flour for breadmaking is bread flour, also called high-gluten flour. The hard winter wheat in this flour is bred to have higher levels of gluten protein.

### All-Purpose Flour

All-purpose is most commonly found in American kitchens. It works for bread but is not ideal. The protein content is lower than that of bread flour, balanced by an equal amount of starch. All-purpose is sometimes used in the beginning of bread recipes that require longer fermentation, taking advantage of its higher starch content as food for yeast.

*All-purpose flour works fine for bread, but it isn't perfect. You can approximate the gluten protein of bread flour by adding gluten flour or vital wheat gluten in the ratio of 1 teaspoon per cup of all-purpose flour.*

## Whole-Wheat Flour

Another member of the wheat flour family is whole wheat. White flour production removes and discards the fibrous bran and nutrient-rich germ, leaving only the inner endosperm, which consists of starch and gluten proteins. Whole-wheat flour retains the bran, germ, and essential nutrients needed for good health. Most large flour production facilities make white flour first, then mix the bran and germ back in to create whole wheat. Stone-ground flours grind the whole grain and keep the flour parts together through the entire process.

Wheat bran and wheat germ are also available separately to add into breads, enhancing flavor and nutrition. Graham is a similar whole-grain wheat flour with a slightly nuttier flavor. White whole-wheat flour is made from a light-colored variety of wheat.

## YEAST

Yeast is the one ingredient that makes bread taste like bread. That characteristic yeastiness is the fragrance you smell as you pull your loaves out of the oven. More importantly, without yeast, your loaves would be less like bread and more like hockey pucks.

Yeast is a living organism that occurs naturally in the air all around you and it comes in different varieties. Yeast feeds on carbohydrates and prefers an environment that is warm and moist. When conditions are right, yeast will feed and produce two byproducts: carbon dioxide and alcohol.

Bubbling foam on the surface of the mixture shows the yeast is working. As carbon dioxide accumulates, the gluten proteins in the dough stretch and the dough rises. The better the conditions, the more carbon dioxide is created and the more the dough will rise. Easily absorbed carbohydrates like sugar or honey get to work quickly. Starches need more time to convert into sugar so the process is slower.

Yeast Maintenance

Because yeast is alive, it can be killed. This happens eventually in the oven but it can happen prematurely if care isn't taken. The first danger yeast encounters is water temperature. Warm water is recommended to get the yeast started but anything over 110°F will kill it. Some bakers use a thermometer for precision but a normal sense of touch works too. You should be able to easily hold your finger in the warm water. That means it's slightly above body temperature (98.6°F). If you can't handle it, the yeast can't either.

Choosing Yeast

The recipes in this chapter call for active dry yeast, which is the most readily available yeast in markets today. There are other options, however. Quick-rise yeast is fed large amounts of phosphorus and ammonia, which speeds up its activity by 50 percent. Instant yeast is coated with ascorbic acid and sugar for immediate activation. Compressed yeast, also known as fresh cake yeast, is the yeast preferred by professionals. It's perishable and, if refrigerated, will hold for about a week. It may also be frozen for several months, although the consistency will change once defrosted.

Similar in consistency to a block of cheese, fresh yeast is more easily measured by weight, which is preferred by production bakers. More importantly, fresh yeast has a superior flavor. It can be used instead of active dry (0.06 ounce is equivalent to 0.25 ounce active dry) in the recipes in this book. Small cakes of yeast are available refrigerated in some markets, although they are often cut with cornstarch. The cornstarch accelerates fermentation but results in a product with less flavor. If you're interested in baking with fresh yeast, try buying a 1-pound block from a local artisan baker. To store it, cut it into sixteen cubes and freeze loose in a Ziploc bag. Pull out ounce-sized blocks as needed.

## WATER

In order for the yeast to absorb nutrients, water must be present. Water can be straight from the tap, bottled, filtered, or purified. Milk, juice, tea, coffee, and eggs are commonly added in place of all or a portion of the water needed. Many bakers insist on a certain type of water based on taste and desired outcome. If your tap water tastes good, it's perfectly fine to use. If you're concerned about the mineral content, use a filter.

Many recipes call for water to be at a certain temperature, the optimal temperature that promotes fermentation, but fermentation takes place even when water is cold. Cool temperatures retard fermentation but don't halt it until a dough is frozen. For this reason, you can slow down production by making a dough in the evening, letting it rise slowly overnight in the fridge, and forming and baking it the following day.

If time allows, a long rise is preferable because more fermentation produces more flavorful bread.

## SALT

While the number one reason that salt is added to any recipe is flavor, salt also plays a chemical role in baking yeast bread. Salt slows and can even stop the process of yeast fermentation. Most dough can withstand salt up to about 2 percent of its weight before the effect becomes detrimental.

Salt also helps toughen gluten by helping bond protein molecules. Salt inhibits enzymes that soften protein, essentially protecting the gluten protein from being destroyed. Dough made without salt will be noticeably slack or mushy and its fermentation will be rapid and unstable. Bread made without salt will have less structure and a bland flavor. Too much salt will prevent the yeast from feeding, causing little, if any, rise. The dough's texture will be tight and it will be too salty to eat. The right amount of salt for an optimal outcome is also the precise amount needed to make bread taste good.

## SUGAR

Sugar makes five major contributions to bread dough. It provides food for the yeast, provides flavor for you, promotes tenderness, preserves crumb, and gives the bread a nice color.

Sugar, like salt, attracts water. This effect is evident in the moistness of a sweet bread as well as in its shelf life. The ability to hold water keeps the bread moist for days longer than a sugar-free bread. The effect of holding water also means excessive amounts of sugar will inhibit fermentation by keeping the water away from where it needs to be. In bread recipes with large amounts of sugar, it must be added in stages to prevent a disruption in fermentation.

When sugar is cooked, it caramelizes. This effect also occurs inside dough, evidenced in the color of a crust. If two bread recipes are made identically but one is made with sugar and one without, the crust of the sugar-free dough will be noticeably pale. It takes a surprisingly small amount of sugar to brown a crust, which is why most recipes contain at least a teaspoon or two. Sweet dough, with double or triple that amount, will be noticeably darker.

### FAT

Fat moistens the bread, tenderizes the crumb, and prolongs shelf life. A lean (fat-free) dough, such as French bread, will begin to stale as soon as it cools and will last less than a day before its drying texture becomes noticeable. Rich dough (dough with fat) remains soft and moist for twice as long.

Fat slows fermentation. Oily dough is heavier, which limits the stretch of the gluten and prevents large pockets of carbon dioxide from forming during fermentation. The absence of large bubbles of gas results in the absence of large holes in the finished bread crumb. Bread with a tight crumb is preferred for recipes such as sandwiches and canapés because it holds in the fillings.

Fat is added to bread dough in several forms, including butter, milk, cream, sour cream, cheese, nut butters, and eggs. Recipes will specify how a fat is to be added, which is usually after the yeast is proofed but before the main quantity of flour is added. It is not necessary to liquefy a solid fat before adding it. Mixing and kneading will add enough friction to warm the fats to a liquid state, making them easily absorbed by the flour.

*Fat and oil are interchangeable; both produce the same effect on the crumb of the dough. The flavors, though, vary greatly. Neutral oils, like vegetable, salad, and canola, are good substitutes for butter. Olive oil has a strong, fruity flavor that isn't always appropriate.*

## Techniques for Success

The ingredients are important, but if you don't know what to do with them, your chances of success are limited. One cannot simply throw everything listed together in a bowl. The proper order of mixing and kneading is key.

### MIXING

Mixing should be done in a large bowl to prevent overflows. The initial mixing can be done with your tool of preference but, for ease of cleanup, a simple dinner fork is the best tool. Spoons don't incorporate ingredients enough and a whisk only works well until flour is added, at which time the dough clumps into the center of the whisk. As soon as the dough holds together, the mass should be turned out onto a lightly floured work surface for kneading.

## KNEADING

Kneading is the most important step in breadmaking. This is the stage when the gluten is created and the dough becomes capable of holding the carbon dioxide that is built up during fermentation. There are many ways to knead but the key is to keep the dough moving around the table. It must be well agitated. Some bakers fold and press, others lift and slap, others roll and drop. As long as it's kept moving for 8–10 minutes, any method will work. As the dough is kneaded, it may be necessary to add more flour.

## THE RIGHT CONSISTENCY

When dough is kneaded, it transforms from a slack, lumpy dough to a tight, smooth one. This transformation is key to the outcome of your bread. After 10 minutes, the dough should be tight and elastic and spring back into shape when poked or stretched. If it doesn't, rest the dough for 5 minutes and check it again. It is possible to over-knead (although this is difficult to do by hand). Over-kneaded dough looks much like under-kneaded dough: lumpy and rough. The difference is the over-kneaded dough will feel tight, not slack.

## KNEADING AND FLOUR

Bread baking is an inexact science and the amount of flour a particular recipe requires depends on several variables, including human error. Air temperature, ingredient temperature, humidity, measurement accuracy, and the type and manufacturer of flour contribute to the amount of flour a recipe will take on any given day. There is only one sure way to know how much is enough, and that's by looking and feeling. The dough should be smooth and soft but not sticky, and not so tough it's hard to knead.

To make a loaf of bread successfully, it's necessary to reserve the last cup of flour called for and add it slowly, a little at a time, as the dough is kneaded. Let each addition work in completely before determining if more is necessary. To reiterate, the dough should be moist and soft but not sticky. Adding a little at a time prevents the over-addition of flour, which makes dough tough, hard to knead, and results in a dry finished product. Sometimes a recipe will require more than what is called for, sometimes less.

### FERMENTATION

Once the dough is kneaded, it must be put up to rise (double). This step is called fermentation and it is when the yeast begins feeding and consequently releases carbon dioxide. If you've kneaded properly, the gas will be trapped within the dough and the bread will rise.

Certain things control fermentation. Yeast likes warmth, so the more warmth you provide (up to about 100°F), the faster the yeast will create gas. Conversely, if you want to slow down the fermentation, you can remove warmth. Therefore, the placement of the rising dough has everything to do with controlling the speed of fermentation.

Set it in a sunny window or near a warm oven and the dough will double in about an hour. The dough is set aside to develop carbon dioxide gas through yeast feeding on carbohydrates. The terms are used interchangeably but most professional bakers consider fermentation the main rise, when the bread doubles in volume.

The dough will rise slowly over a period of 8–10 hours. The slower, chilled method is ideal for busy cooks who may not have time to make a dough from start to finish in one day. Fermentation stops completely below 32°F, which makes the freezer a great place to store dough for extended periods. Defrost frozen dough in the fridge for even results.

*What's the difference between proofing and fermenting? The proof is the final short rise just before baking.*

## FORMING

Before a loaf can be baked, it must first be formed. Each recipe in this book includes a suggestion for form but most doughs can easily be made in a variety of shapes. There are two key points to remember when forming a loaf. First, the dough should be tight, smooth, and free of air pockets. This is achieved by rolling, flattening, and folding as the dough is formed. The more a dough is worked, the tighter and more elastic the gluten will become. Second, the forming should be done fairly quickly because, as long as the dough is unbaked and unfrozen, fermentation will continue. As the dough sits, gases build, gluten relaxes, and the loaf will lose its shape.

If the form is not to your liking, the process can easily be repeated, but the dough must rest for about 5 minutes first. Resting relaxes the gluten, allowing for more gas to build up, thus softening the dough and making it easy to form once again.

## The Baking Processes

You don't need to know what happens in the oven to make delicious fresh bread, but having an idea of what steps your dough goes through will help you troubleshoot bad loaves. In the heat of the oven, several events take place. They don't happen simultaneously but slowly, each peaking at certain temperatures.

### GAS EXPANDS

The first noticeable change is the expansion of gases. A loaf will puff up quickly, within a few minutes. This effect is known as "oven spring." In yeast breads, carbon dioxide expands through the fermentation process. In quick breads, carbon dioxide expands, too, but is created by chemical leaveners (baking soda or baking powder). In soufflés and sponge cakes, air expands during the whipping of eggs. This expansion pushes the dough up and raises the bread until the proteins solidify and form a crust.

## PROTEINS SOLIDIFY

When proteins solidify, they react just like an egg in a hot frying pan, changing from something soft to something firm. This change creates the structure of bread as we know it. Heat causes the chains of amino acids to tighten, altering the overall structures of the proteins. The most common proteins present in bread include gluten, egg, and dairy proteins.

## SUGARS CARAMELIZE

Heat melts sugar and turns it brown in a process called caramelization. The higher the heat, the faster the caramelization takes place. This is not always a good thing because the crust shouldn't brown before the interior is cooked. Therefore, oven temperatures should be adjusted in accordance with the size of the loaf being baked. Rolls can be baked at high temperatures because heat will penetrate quickly, usually before the crust caramelizes. In a large loaf, more time is required for the heat to penetrate to the center and cook it. Unless the temperature is lowered, the crust will be well browned long before the loaf is ready.

## FATS MELT

Fats melt and liquefy in the oven, allowing them to be absorbed. If butter is not fully incorporated, either by accident or on purpose, it will melt away, leaving an air pocket. Care should be taken when fermenting rich doughs. Fats start melting with very little heat and if the dough gets too warm, the fat will run out of it, resulting in a greasy dough that is much harder to form into a loaf. Loss of fat also makes the bread less delicious.

## WATER EVAPORATES

Water evaporation in a loaf of bread is most easily observed by the weight of the finished product. A properly cooked loaf will be noticeably lighter in weight than the raw dough because the water has evaporated. The hollow sound you listen for when determining whether a loaf is done is the echo from the hollow spaces that were once filled with water.

Water evaporation is also apparent in the making of biscuits and other recipes that use the cut-in method. Butter contains a large percentage of water and because the butter in a cut-in dough is left in small chunks, the evaporation of its water creates steam that pushes up the dough, creating little pockets of air and a flaky texture. The same effect occurs in flaky pie dough and puff pastries.

## STARCHES GELATINIZE

Oven heat causes starch to gelatinize. Just as cornstarch can thicken a sauce, natural starch in flour will thicken when moistened and heated. The starch is the part of flour that is not gluten protein, which means there is abundant gelatinization in everything baked with grain. This thickening plays a major role in creating the texture of the finished crumb. Starch gives structure while remaining flexible and soft. Without starch, bread would be hard and tough.

## DONENESS

Recipes provide a cooking time, but the actual time it takes to completely bake a loaf can vary tremendously. The size of the oven, the size of the loaves, the thickness and material of the pans, recipe accuracy, ingredient variation, and the number of items in the oven at one time all affect baking time. The only sure way to judge doneness is by sight and feel.

A finished loaf should be golden brown in color. It should also feel lighter coming out than it was going in and make a hollow sound when thumped. The internal temperature of a bread can be taken to determine doneness as well. Insert an instant-read thermometer into the thickest part of the loaf. The internal temperature should be in the range of 200°F–210°F when cooked.

## Essential Tools of the Trade

In the past, people would bake bread with only the essential equipment: a bowl, a fork, a pan, and an oven. You can do the same. Here's what you need to know about basic breadmaking equipment.

### PANS

Most breads can be baked on a simple baking sheet. In a professional kitchen, these pans are called sheet pans. They are made of heavy aluminum and have a ½" lip. These pans are indispensable to a baker and are used for just about everything. Some breads require a loaf pan and the market is flooded with a plethora from which to choose. Heaviest is best, made from glass, ceramic, thick aluminum, or cast iron. These materials hold and spread heat evenly and reduce the chance of a burnt crust. Thin baking pans will cause bread to burn, especially when used for breads that require long baking times. The same criterion applies to muffin pans.

*Regardless of the type of pan chosen, the dough should always be placed into it seam-side down. This means when the loaf is formed, the smooth, tight, seamless side of the dough should face up, and any rough, folded, or pleated skin should face down in the pan. The weight of the dough on these seams keeps them from opening in an unattractive way.*

OVENS

Any standard oven is suitable for baking bread. The convection oven is a common appliance in many homes but can be a little tricky for the new baker. Convection ovens were created to promote even browning of foods. They are not as successful at even browning as they are at increasing the speed of baking.

Convection ovens contain fans that move air throughout the oven cavity, resulting in an increased temperature. This is very convenient for small items like cookies and muffins but larger loaves of bread need more time for the heat to penetrate the dough. Convection baking usually results in a burnt crust and doughy center.

Some convection ovens have a switch that turns the fans on and off. For large items, the fans should be turned off and the oven used in the conventional manner. If the oven doesn't have an on-off capability, consider baking smaller breads such as rolls or baking them in a high-sided pan that can be covered in foil to prevent the moving air from reaching the loaf.

## ADDITIONAL TOOLS

Following are some additional items you might find helpful in baking.

### Baskets

Europeans have long used cane baskets called banneton or brotformen to ferment bread. They promote an even, uniform bowl shape, which is higher and rounder than a loaf proofed on a flat baking sheet. Dusted with flour, the cane leaves a decorative impression on the proofing breads. Some of these baskets are lined with linen, which needs less flour to prevent sticking. Breads are turned out of the baskets onto a baking sheet or peel before going into the oven.

A proofing linen cloth, called a cloche, is sometimes used for baguettes for the same purpose. The cloth is a simple rectangle pleated in between each loaf to shape the dough as it's proofed.

### Parchment Paper

Parchment serves many purposes, including preventing baked goods from sticking to pans. Used as a pan liner, parchment not only eases removal of the finished product but also promotes even browning and uniform texture of the crust. In addition, parchment extends the lifetime of bakeware. Lined with paper, pans don't come into contact with ingredients. If they did, these ingredients would burn in the oven, leaving the pan with a coating of oil and carbon. These deposits weaken the pan, as does the excessive scrubbing needed to remove them. In addition, pans left with food deposits will warp, bend, and buckle in the oven where heat flow is interrupted.

Parchment is also useful for wrapping and storage. It is frequently used by professionals to hold ingredients and can be formed into a cone for decorating.

### Racks

Cooling racks are an important last step in the production of bread. If bread is allowed to cool without a rack, condensation (also known as bread sweat) will form underneath, resulting in a soggy bottom crust. A rack allows air to circulate underneath, releasing steam and evaporating any condensation for a dry, crisp crust. A rack should leave at least ¼" of space between the bread and the counter.

## Classic Recipes

Now that you know the fundamentals of bread baking, try it out with these simple and delicious bread recipes.

## PRAIRIE WHITE

*When using cool liquid, bread dough will require a longer fermentation. The outcome is a heartier, more rustic flavor, commonly referred to as country-style.*

### Yields 1 loaf

| | |
|---|---|
| 1 cup cold buttermilk | 2 tablespoons canola oil |
| 2 tablespoons honey | 1½ teaspoons kosher salt |
| 1¾ teaspoons (1 package) active dry yeast | 3–4 cups bread flour |
| | 1 tablespoon cornmeal |
| 1 large egg | 2 tablespoons cream |

1. In a large bowl, combine buttermilk, honey, and yeast. Stir to dissolve and let stand until foamy, about 30 minutes.
2. Add egg, oil, salt, and 1 cup flour; stir to combine. Add enough remaining flour to create a firm dough. Turn out onto a floured surface and knead 8–10 minutes. Return to bowl, dust the top lightly with flour, and cover with a damp cloth or plastic wrap. Let rise at room temperature until doubled in volume, about 3 hours.
3. Line a baking sheet with parchment; dust with cornmeal. Turn risen dough onto a floured surface and shape into a smooth, round ball. Place onto prepared baking sheet seam-side down. Cover loosely with plastic and set aside to proof for 30 minutes. Preheat oven to 375°F.
4. Brush cream lightly over risen loaf. Using a serrated knife, slash a crosshatch design into the top of the dough about 1" deep. Place a pan of cold water at the bottom of the oven to create steam. Bake until golden brown and hollow sounding, about 30–40 minutes. Remove to a rack and cool completely.

# 3-GRAIN BROWN LOAF

*This dough makes a satisfying dark loaf perfect for sandwiches. It makes great rolls as well. Be sure to use rolled oats in this recipe, not quick-cooking oats.*

**Yields 2 loaves**

1¾ cups warm milk
¼ cup plus 1 tablespoon molasses, divided
1¾ teaspoons (1 package) active dry yeast
2 tablespoons canola oil
1 tablespoon cocoa powder

1 cup whole-wheat flour
1 cup rye flour
1 cup rolled oats
1½ teaspoons kosher salt
3–4 cups bread flour
1 tablespoon hot water

1. In a large bowl, combine milk, ¼ cup molasses, and yeast. Stir to dissolve and let stand until foamy, about 10 minutes.
2. Add oil, cocoa, whole-wheat flour, rye flour, and oats; stir to combine. Add salt and enough bread flour to create a firm dough. Add flour as needed to reduce stickiness. Turn out onto a floured surface and knead 8–10 minutes. Return to bowl, dust the top with flour, and cover with a damp cloth or plastic wrap. Let rise at room temperature until doubled in volume, about 2 hours.
3. Coat two 9" × 5" loaf pans with pan spray and line the bottom and short sides with a strip of parchment. Turn risen dough onto a floured surface, divide into two equal portions, and shape into oblong loaves. Place into prepared pans seam-side down, cover loosely with plastic wrap, and set aside to proof for 30 minutes or until dough rises above the pans. Preheat oven to 375°F.
4. Combine remaining 1 tablespoon molasses with 1 tablespoon hot water and brush gently onto the risen dough. Bake until golden brown and hollow sounding, about 30–40 minutes. Cool 10 minutes, remove loaves from pans, and cool completely on a rack.

# SOURDOUGH STARTER

*The longer you keep this starter going, the better your bread will be. There are stories about sourdough starters that have survived for over a hundred years, passed down from generation to generation.*

**Yields 9 cups**

**3 cups water, divided**
**⅛ teaspoon active dry yeast**

**3 cups all-purpose flour, divided**

1. **Day 1:** Combine 1 cup water, yeast, and 1 cup flour in a ceramic or glass bowl. Stir to combine, cover loosely with damp cheesecloth or towel, and set aside at room temperature. Stir this mixture once a day for the next three days.
2. **Day 4:** To the starter, add 1 cup water and 1 cup flour. Stir well, cover again, and set aside at room temperature for another four days, stirring once a day as before.
3. **Day 8:** Again, add 1 cup water and 1 cup flour. Mix thoroughly. Let stand at room temperature loosely covered for 6 hours or until the starter foams and doubles in volume. The starter is now ready to use. To keep your starter alive, replace the quantity that has been used with an equal amount of water and flour (for every 1 cup used, replace with ½ cup water and ½ cup flour). Keep covered, stir every day, and feed every five days by removing some starter and again replacing it with an equal amount of water and flour. If you don't wish to feed it but want to keep it, cover airtight and refrigerate indefinitely, taking it out and repeating the process (removing and replacing 1 cup as before) for ten days before using it again.

# SOURDOUGH BOULE

Boule *literally means "ball," and indeed these loaves are golden spheres of delectable goodness.*

**Yields 2 loaves**

1 cup Sourdough Starter (see recipe in this chapter)
1 cup water, divided
1¾ teaspoons (1 package) active dry yeast

1 cup all-purpose flour
1 teaspoon kosher salt
3–4 cups bread flour
2 tablespoons cornmeal

1. To make the sponge, combine Sourdough Starter, ½ cup water, and yeast in a large bowl. Stir to dissolve and let stand 5 minutes. Add all-purpose flour and beat 1 minute. Cover and let stand at room temperature 8–12 hours.
2. To the sponge, add remaining ½ cup water, salt, and enough bread flour to make a soft dough. Turn out onto a floured work surface and knead 8–10 minutes. Add flour as needed to reduce stickiness. Return to bowl, dust with flour, cover with plastic, and let rise at room temperature until doubled in volume, about 1½ hours.
3. Line a baking sheet with parchment and sprinkle with cornmeal. Turn risen dough onto a floured surface and divide into two equal portions. Roll into balls and place on prepared pan, seam-side down. Dust generously with flour, cover again with plastic, and let rise until doubled, about 30 minutes. Preheat oven to 475°F.
4. Using a serrated knife, slice decorative slash marks into the surface of the dough about ½" deep. Place a pan of cold water at the bottom of the oven to create steam. Bake until golden brown and hollow sounding, about 30–40 minutes. Cool completely on a rack.

# FLAKY PIE CRUST

*This recipe is best for pies where the crust is blind-baked, such as with cream pies, or used as the top crust for fruit pies. This also works beautifully for a lattice top.*

**Yields 1 (9") crust**

1¼ cups all-purpose flour
2 tablespoons sugar
½ teaspoon salt
6 tablespoons butter, cubed
   and chilled

2 tablespoons lard or vegetable
   shortening, chilled
2–4 tablespoons ice water

1. In a large bowl, sift together the flour, sugar, and salt.
2. Add the chilled fats and rub them into the flour mixture with your fingers until 30 percent of the fat is between pea- and hazelnut-sized and the rest is blended in well.
3. Add 2 tablespoons water and mix until the dough forms a rough ball. Add more water, 1 tablespoon at a time, if needed.
4. Turn the dough out onto a lightly floured surface and form a disk. Wrap in plastic and chill at least 30 minutes or up to three days.
5. Remove the dough from the refrigerator about 10 minutes before rolling out. Roll out on a lightly floured surface to a ⅛"-thick 12" circle, turning the dough often to make sure it doesn't stick. Dust the surface with additional flour if needed.
6. Place the crust into a 9" pie plate and chill 30 minutes before use.

# MEALY PIE CRUST

*Mealy Pie Crusts are best used as the bottom crust for fruit pies and custard pies.*

**Yields 1 (9") crust**

1¼ cups all-purpose flour
2 tablespoons sugar
½ teaspoon salt
4 tablespoons butter, cubed
  and chilled

¼ cup lard or vegetable
  shortening, chilled
2–4 tablespoons ice water

1. In a large bowl, sift together the flour, sugar, and salt.
2. Add the butter and shortening to the bowl and rub the fat into the flour with your fingers until the mixture looks like coarse sand with no large pieces of fat remaining.
3. Add 2 tablespoons water and mix until the dough forms a rough ball. Add more water, 1 tablespoon at a time, if needed.
4. Turn the dough out onto a lightly floured surface and form a disk. Wrap in plastic and chill at least 30 minutes or up to three days.
5. Remove the dough from the refrigerator about 10 minutes before rolling out. Roll out on a lightly floured surface to a ⅛"-thick 12" circle, turning the dough often to make sure it doesn't stick. Dust the surface with additional flour if needed.
6. Fold the dough in half and place into a 9" pie plate. Unfold and carefully push the dough into the pan. Use kitchen scissors or a paring knife to trim the dough to 1" beyond the pan's edge.
7. Cover with plastic and chill until ready to bake.

# LATTICE-TOP CHERRY PIE

*If fresh cherries are available, feel free to use them here. A few toasted flaked almonds make an excellent garnish.*

**Serves 8**

*20 ounces frozen pitted cherries*
*1 cup sugar*
*½ cup cornstarch*
*1 tablespoon butter*
*¼ teaspoon salt*
*1 teaspoon lemon juice*
*¼ teaspoon almond extract*

*1 (9") Mealy Pie Crust, unbaked (see recipe in this chapter)*
*1 Flaky Pie Crust, unbaked, cut into 10 (1") strips (see recipe in this chapter)*
*1 large egg, beaten*

1. Heat oven to 375°F.
2. Thaw the cherries and drain the juices into a measuring cup. Add enough water to the juice to equal ½ cup.
3. In a small saucepan, combine the juice, sugar, and cornstarch until smooth. Cook over medium heat until the mixture begins to boil and thicken.
4. Add the butter, salt, lemon juice, and almond extract. Mix well then fold in the cherries. Cool to room temperature.
5. Pour into the Mealy Pie Crust and top with the pastry strips. Lay out five strips of pie dough on top of the filling about ½" apart. Starting ½" from the edge of the pie, fold back every other strip and lay down one strip of pastry. Fold the pastry back down and fold back the other pieces. Lay down a second strip about ½" from the first strip. Repeat this process until all the strips are used. Trim the dough to 1" beyond the pan's edge. Tuck the edge of the top crust under the edge of the bottom crust. Crimp the dough using your fingers or a fork. Brush the lattice with beaten egg.
6. Bake 40–45 minutes or until the filling is bubbly in the center and the lattice is golden brown. Cool 30 minutes before serving.

# CREAM CHEESE PASTRY CRUST

*This is a very rich, tender dough that is lovely for fruit and nut pies.*

**Yields 1 (9") crust**

½ cup cream cheese, room
    temperature
½ cup butter, room temperature
1 teaspoon lemon zest

1½ cups all-purpose flour
¼ cup sugar
½ teaspoon salt
¼ teaspoon baking powder

1. In a large mixing bowl, cream together the cream cheese, butter, and lemon zest until smooth.
2. In a separate medium bowl, sift together the flour, sugar, salt, and baking powder. Add the sifted dry ingredients into the cream cheese mixture and stir until it forms a soft dough. If the mixture feels sticky, add more flour, 1 tablespoon at a time, until it is smooth and no longer sticky.
3. Turn the dough out onto a lightly floured surface and form a disk. Wrap in plastic and chill at least 1 hour or up to three days.
4. Remove the dough from the refrigerator for 10 minutes to warm up. Roll out on a lightly floured surface to a ⅛"-thick 12" circle, turning the dough often to make sure it doesn't stick. Dust the surface with additional flour if needed.
5. Fold the dough in half and place into a 9" pie plate. Unfold and carefully press the dough into the pan. Use kitchen scissors or a paring knife to trim the dough to 1" beyond the pan's edge.
6. Cover with plastic and chill until ready to bake.

# CHESS PIE

*Originally from England, Chess Pie is now a staple in the southern part of the United States. The filling is very rich.*

**Serves 8**

*4 large eggs*
*1 stick butter, melted*
*1 cup sugar*
*1 tablespoon yellow cornmeal*
*1 teaspoon vanilla extract*

*½ cup whole milk*
*1 tablespoon fresh lemon juice*
*1 (9") Cream Cheese Pastry Crust, unbaked (see recipe in this chapter)*

1. Heat the oven to 350°F.
2. In a large bowl, whisk together the eggs, butter, and sugar until smooth. Add the cornmeal, vanilla, milk, and lemon juice. Whisk until well combined.
3. Pour the mixture into the pastry crust and place on a baking sheet. Bake 50–55 minutes or until the filling is set and the top is golden brown. Allow to cool to room temperature before serving.

# PUMPKIN PIE

*Filled with warm spices and creamy pumpkin, this traditional pie is a perfect ending to a Thanksgiving or holiday meal.*

**Serves 8**

¾ cup sugar
1 teaspoon ground cinnamon
½ teaspoon salt
¼ teaspoon allspice
¼ teaspoon ground cloves
⅛ teaspoon fresh grated nutmeg

2 large eggs
15 ounces pumpkin purée
12 ounces evaporated milk
1 (9") Cream Cheese Pastry Crust, unbaked (see recipe in this chapter)

1. Heat the oven to 425°F.
2. In a large bowl, whisk together the sugar, cinnamon, salt, allspice, cloves, and nutmeg until well combined.
3. Add the eggs, pumpkin, and evaporated milk and whisk until smooth.
4. Pour the mixture into the prepared pastry crust and place on a baking sheet. Bake in the lower third of the oven for 15 minutes, then reduce the heat to 350°F and bake an additional 40–45 minutes or until the filling is set at the edges and just slightly wobbly in the center. Cool 3 hours on a wire rack before slicing.

# CLASSIC OATMEAL COOKIES

*These are the chewy, old-fashioned oatmeal cookies you remember from childhood. Leave them plain or add any (or all!) of the optional ingredients—they are delicious any way you make them. Be careful not to overbake.*

**Yields 60 cookies**

¾ **cup vegetable shortening**
1 **cup packed brown sugar**
½ **cup granulated sugar**
1 **large egg**
1 **teaspoon vanilla extract**
¼ **cup water**
3 **cups old-fashioned oatmeal, uncooked**

1 **cup flour**
1 **teaspoon salt**
½ **teaspoon baking soda**
1 **cup coconut flakes (optional)**
1 **cup raisins (optional)**
1 **cup pecans or walnuts (optional)**

1. Preheat oven to 350°F. Lightly grease cookie sheets.
2. In a large mixing bowl, beat together shortening and sugars until light and fluffy. Beat in egg, vanilla, and water.
3. In a separate large bowl, combine oatmeal, flour, salt, and baking soda, then stir into creamed mixture. Add coconut, raisin, and nuts if using.
4. Drop by rounded teaspoons about 2" apart onto prepared cookie sheets. Bake 12–15 minutes.
5. Allow to cool 5 minutes before removing from cookie sheet.

# CHOCOLATE TOFFEE COOKIES

*These huge cookies are rich and full of buttery toffee flavor. They're a bit like a brownie and a bit like a cookie. Watch them carefully; the bottoms burn easily.*

**Yields 18 cookies**

¾ cup all-purpose flour
1 teaspoon baking powder
⅛ teaspoon salt
1 pound bittersweet chocolate, chopped
¼ cup unsalted butter
2 cups packed brown sugar

4 large eggs
1 tablespoon vanilla extract
1 teaspoon butter flavoring
1½ cups coarsely chopped Heath bars
1 cup chopped and toasted almonds

1. In a medium bowl, combine flour, baking powder, and salt. Set aside.
2. In a medium saucepan over low heat, melt chocolate and butter together. Cool to room temperature.
3. In a large mixing bowl, beat sugar and eggs until thick, about 5 minutes. Add vanilla, butter flavoring, and chocolate mixture.
4. Stir in dry ingredients, blending well. Fold in Heath bars and almonds. Cover and chill overnight.
5. Next day, preheat oven to 350°F. Line a baking sheet with parchment paper.
6. Drop cookies by ¼ cup scoops 3" apart on baking sheets. Bake 15 minutes or until tops are dry and cracked but not overdone. Cool completely.

## SOUR CREAM SUGAR COOKIES

*These cookies are a soft and cake-like—but not too sweet—drop sugar cookie. These are very easy to make, with no rolling or cutting. The best size ice cream scoops to use for drop cookie dough like this are #80 or #100. Scoop the dough out of the bowl with the scoop, pressing the dough firmly into it. Release the dough onto the prepared cookie sheet. Each cookie will be uniform in size and texture because they will bake at the same rate.*

**Yields 60 cookies**

5 cups cake flour
1 teaspoon baking soda
2 teaspoons baking powder
¼ teaspoon freshly grated
   nutmeg
½ teaspoon salt

1 cup unsalted butter
1 cup sugar
2 large eggs, room temperature
1 teaspoon vanilla extract
2 cups sour cream

1. Preheat oven to 375°F. Grease cookie sheets.
2. In a medium bowl, sift cake flour, baking soda, baking powder, nutmeg, and salt together. Set aside.
3. In a large mixing bowl, cream butter and sugar until fluffy. Beat in eggs and vanilla.
4. Add flour mixture and sour cream alternately to mixture until well combined. Drop dough by ice cream scoop (or teaspoon, if you don't have an ice cream scoop) about 2" apart on prepared cookie sheets.
5. Bake 12–15 minutes until golden. Allow to cool a few minutes on cookie sheets before removing to cool completely.

**CHAPTER 4**

# HERBAL REMEDIES

Herbal medicine is the practice of using one or more parts of a plant—its seeds, berries, roots, leaves, bark, or flowers—to relieve physical and psychological problems, prevent disease, or simply improve overall health and vitality. Herbal remedies are part of the cottagecore movement as they emphasize natural and simple forms of medicine over the overly processed, manufactured, and oftentimes dangerous chemical alternatives. Herbs have a long history of use in the medical field and, when used properly, are safe and powerful medicines. This chapter will explain a few types of herbal remedies and guide you through creating some of your own to battle various common ailments.

## Using Herbs for Healing

To use herbs safely and effectively, follow these guidelines:

- **Start slowly.** Take the smallest dose that's sensible, then see how you feel. Nothing? Take a bit more. Remember that herbs are almost always gentler and less potent than their pharmaceutical counterparts, so you don't want a dramatic reaction. If you're using an herb that can produce side effects, exercise more restraint in increasing your dose than if you're using a more innocuous herb. You should also be more careful about upping the dose if you're treating a senior or child.
- **Research.** Before taking an herb, research the condition you're treating, including the various treatment options—herbal and conventional—and the benefits of each.
- **Don't overdo it.** Adverse reactions from the herbal remedies used most often today are extremely rare, but they can happen—usually when an herb is overused. If you take too much for too long, you can have problems.
- **Be a patient patient.** Because herbs work subtly, they have what's known as a long onset of action. Unlike a pharmaceutical painkiller, for example, a dose of willow (*Salix alba*) won't get rid of your headache in a half-hour.
- **Take the long view.** The general rule is to give an herbal remedy a few weeks before deciding if it's working or not.
- **Don't use short-term remedies for long-term problems.** If you find yourself constantly reaching for the same type of

acute remedy, it's time to change tactics. Contact a professional who can help you address the underlying problem.

## DOSAGES

When using store-bought herbs, always follow the manufacturer's guidelines. When you don't have any—the package doesn't have dosage information or you've made the remedy yourself—you can use these.

For chronic conditions, adults should take the following doses:

- Tea: 3–4 cups a day
- Tincture or syrup: ½–1 teaspoon three times a day

For acute problems, adults should take the following until symptoms subside:

- Tea: ¼–½ cup every hour or two, up to 3 cups a day
- Tincture or syrup: ¼–½ teaspoon every 30–60 minutes

The dosages given here are for nonconcentrated products. Because commercial herbal extracts vary widely in their concentrations, the best advice for taking a concentrated extract is to check the product's concentration level and divide that by the dosages recommended here. Generally speaking, seniors should take a quarter of an adult dose.

Here are two formulas for determining the best dosage for a child:

- Take your child's age and add 12, then divide the child's age by this total. So if your child is four, you would do: 4+12 = 16. 4 divided by 16 = 0.25, or ¼ of the adult dosage.
- Divide the number of the child's age at next birthday by 24. So a three-year-old child who would be turning four would be: 4 divided by 24 = .16, or ⅙ the adult dosage.

Using these formulas, a six-year-old would get roughly a third of an adult dose and a twelve-year-old would get roughly half. If you're treating a baby younger than six months and you're breastfeeding, you can take the appropriate herb yourself, passing it to your baby via your breastmilk.

## KEEPING AN HERBAL MEDICINE BOX

With only a few common tools and a few simple ingredients available at most herb shops or natural food stores, you can make your own herbal remedies. By making your own, you can control more aspects of the product you're using and you'll gain a greater understanding of the power of plants.

Here are a few things to keep in mind when making your own remedies:

- Herbs and herbal preparations do best when they're stored in airtight glass jars out of direct light in a cool area. Light, oxygen, and heat can degrade them.
- Never use aluminum pots or containers; aluminum can react with the herbs. Stick to glass, ceramic, stainless steel, or cast iron.

- Store all remedies and ingredients—especially essential oils and alcohol-based tinctures—out of children's reach. Many essential oils are extremely toxic, even in very small doses.

## Types of Herbal Remedies

There are several ways you can make herbs into herbal remedies. You can make them into teas and tinctures for oral use or oils and balms for external application. The following sections will explain these basic types of remedies and even give you a few recipes to battle some common problems.

### THERAPEUTIC TEAS

A tea is, without question, the simplest of herbal remedies to prepare and use. Even the most inexperienced of cooks can boil water, and that's really all it takes to make a cup of tea.

To make a tea with loose herbs, put the plant material into a strainer and the strainer into a cup, then fill the cup with boiling water. Cover the cup; the medicinal value of many herbs, including peppermint (*Mentha × piperita*), is contained in the essential oils, so you'll want to keep the steam from escaping. You can also make an infusion using a French coffee press, just don't use the same one you use to make coffee.

When making tea, use about 1 teaspoon of dried herbs per cup of water. Steep for 15 minutes or longer. The more herb you use and the longer you let it steep, the stronger your tea will be.

## SWEET-TASTING SYRUPS

Syrups are a great way to treat children with herbs. They're sweet and go down much easier than other liquid remedies. If properly stored, syrups will last for several weeks. To make an herbal syrup, first make a quart of an herbal tea, then simmer it down and mix with honey or another sweetener (like maple syrup or brown sugar).

*Experts advise against giving raw (unpasteurized) honey to children younger than a year old due to the risk of botulism. If you're making syrup to give to a baby, replace honey with commercial maple syrup or brown sugar.*

## TINCTURES

Tinctures are liquid herbal extracts made by combining herbs with a solvent. Traditional tinctures are made with a beverage alcohol but you can also use vinegar or vegetable glycerin (available at many health food stores) instead. Tinctures are typically more potent than infusions, decoctions (an infusion using the hard or woody parts of the plant), or syrups. Here's some advice on making your own tinctures:

- Start with bulk herbs (fresh is best) and chop them finely. Put them in a clean glass jar and add enough alcohol—80- or

100-proof vodka, gin, or brandy—to cover them with about 2" or 3" of fluid. Cover with a tight-fitting lid, place in a warm, dark spot, and leave it there for four to six weeks—the longer, the better.

- Once a day, shake the jar to keep the herbs from settling at the bottom.
- When the time is up, strain the herbs and discard them. Transfer the tincture to a small glass bottle (ideally one with a dropper to make it easier to get the right dose). Stored properly, it will keep for two years or longer. Be sure to keep tinctures out of the reach of children.

## INFUSED OILS

Herbal oils can be used alone or as a base for creams or ointments. There are two ways to make infused oils: using the sun or using a stove. You can use many types of vegetable oil as your base—coconut (*Cocos nucifera*) and almond (*Prunus dulcis*) are popular choices—then add an equal amount of cocoa (*Theobroma cacao*) butter to thicken the mixture, if you like (best with the stovetop method).

### Making Solar-Infused Oils

Place a handful of dried herbs in a clean, clear glass jar and fill it with oil (you'll use about 2 ounces [8 tablespoons] of herbs per pint of oil). Cover tightly and place in a warm, sunny spot. Leave it there for two weeks. When the time is up, pour the mixture through a piece of cheesecloth or muslin, making sure to wring the cloth tightly to catch every last drop of oil.

Discard the herbs and replace them with a new batch, then let the oil and herbs steep for another two weeks. Transfer to clean glass bottles. Stored correctly, infused oils will last several months.

*When making infused oils, you'll get the best results with dried herbs. Plant material that contains too much moisture can cause the oil to get moldy. (Your oil can also grow mold if it's made or stored in a jar with an ill-fitting lid, which can allow moisture to get in.)*

### Making Oils on the Stove

If you don't have a lot of sunshine (or a month to wait), you can make your oil on the stove using a double boiler. Put the herbs and oil in the top section, then fill the bottom section with water and bring it to a low boil. Let the oil simmer gently for 30–60 minutes, checking frequently to make sure the oil isn't overheating (it will start to smoke if that's the case). The lower and longer you let it simmer, the better your oil will be.

### HERBAL OINTMENTS

Ointments, also known as salves, are thick, oil-based preparations used to treat superficial wounds (like scrapes, burns, and insect bites) and soothe aching muscles and joints. Here's how to make them:

1. Start with an infused oil that's been strained. Put the oil into a small pan and add grated beeswax—¼ cup per cup of infused oil. Heat on low until the beeswax is completely melted, then remove from the heat.
2. Test a small amount for consistency by putting it into the freezer for a minute or two to cool it. If it seems too hard (you can't spread it easily), heat it again and add more oil. If it's too oily, reheat and add more beeswax.
3. When you've got the consistency you want, transfer the ointment to clean glass jars. Stored properly, ointments will last several months.

## COMPRESSES

Compresses are small bundles of material that have been soaked in an infusion or decoction and applied to the skin. Linen, gauze, and cotton are often used for compresses. Make sure the infusion or decoction is hot when you soak the material. Apply the compress to the affected area and change it once it cools down.

## POULTICE

When you make a poultice, you wrap the herbs themselves in a piece of gauze and soak it in the infusion or decoction, then apply it to the skin. You can also use cider vinegar in place of the usual water when you create an infusion or decoction for poultice use. Apply it to the affected area and change it once it cools down.

## Treating Burns and Sunburns

A burn is an injury to the skin that can be caused by several things, including heat, chemicals, sun exposure, and electricity. Most burns are minor—you've accidentally touched a hot stove or spent too much time in the sun—and can be treated at home. Here are some herbal remedies for minor burns or sunburns (for more serious second- and third-degree burns, see your health-care provider):

- **Aloe (*Aloe vera*):** The gel from this cactus-like plant is legendary as a burn remedy. Research shows it improves circulation in superficial blood vessels, inhibits inflammation, and promotes tissue repair.
- **Calendula (*Calendula officinalis*):** Calendula, aka pot marigold, has both astringent and anti-inflammatory properties and is another classic burn remedy. Studies show it also has anti-edema, analgesic, and wound-healing properties.
- **Lavender (*Lavandula angustifolia*):** The essential oil of lavender is a gentle anesthetic and anti-inflammatory with skin-healing capabilities. Research shows it can relieve swelling and pain in minor burns.
- **Saint John's wort (*Hypericum perforatum*):** Saint John's wort is used topically to treat burns and other superficial skin injuries. It possesses antimicrobial, antioxidant, and anti-inflammatory constituents, and research shows it can modulate the immune response to burns to speed healing.

(Ironically, taking Saint John's wort orally can increase your susceptibility to sunburn, so be sure to use sunblock.)

- **Witch-hazel (*Hamamelis virginiana*):** Witch-hazel is a cooling, soothing remedy for burns (and all types of cuts, scrapes, and other skin injuries). Research shows it can reduce skin inflammation caused by sunburns. It also works as a styptic (it stops bleeding).

## BURN OINTMENT RECIPE

Here is a classic burn ointment remedy that combines skin-soothing, inflammation-fighting, and germ-killing herbs. Keep this ointment around the house for cooking mishaps.

**You will need:**
- 1 part calendula (*Calendula officinalis*) flowers
- 1 part comfrey (*Symphytum officinale*) leaves
- 1 part comfrey (*Symphytum officinale*) root
- 1 part Saint John's wort (*Hypericum perforatum*) flowers
- 1 part olive (*Olea europaea*) oil
- Beeswax, grated

**Directions**
1. Put the calendula flowers, comfrey leaves and root, and Saint John's wort flowers into the top section of a double boiler along with the olive oil. Fill the bottom with water and bring it to a low boil.

2. Let the oil simmer gently for 30–60 minutes, checking frequently to make sure the oil isn't overheating (it will start to smoke if that's the case).

3. Strain the oil, put it into a small pan, and add grated beeswax—¼ cup per cup of infused oil. Heat on low until the beeswax is completely melted, then remove from the heat.

4. Test a small amount for consistency by putting it into the freezer for 1–2 minutes to cool it. If it seems too hard (you can't spread it easily), heat it again and add more oil. If it's too oily, reheat and add more beeswax.

5. When you've got the consistency you want, transfer the ointment to clean glass jars. Stored properly, ointments will last several months.

## Easing Itching and Scratching

Plenty of things you encounter both at home and away can cause irritation and itching: bites and stings from insects as well as an inadvertent brush against a toxic plant. Poison ivy, oak, and sumac contain oils that can cause an itchy, red rash, often involving blisters. (You can even have a reaction if you touch something—an article of clothing, your dog's fur—that's touched the plant or if you inhale smoke from a fire that contains it.)

Several species of bugs—including bees, wasps, and hornets—can sting you, leaving behind venom and sometimes a stinger, plus a welt that's itchy, painful, or both. Biting insects, such as ticks, spiders, fleas, and mosquitoes, like to take away something (usually a bit of blood) and leave a bit of saliva that creates a reaction (usually itching and inflammation) in return.

## HERBAL REMEDIES FOR ITCHING

- **Echinacea (*Echinacea purpurea*):** Used topically, echinacea is a mild anesthetic and antiseptic that fights infection and speeds healing. In the lab, it's been shown to reduce inflammation and swelling better than a topical NSAID.
- **Eucalyptus (*Eucalyptus globulus*):** Eucalyptus oil works as a topical antiseptic and painkiller; it can relieve pain and itching, speed healing, and prevent infection.
- **Sangre de grado (*Croton lechleri*):** This South American tree is known for its anti-inflammatory and wound-healing prowess. Research shows it can relieve pain and itching caused by all sorts of insects—including fire ants, wasps, and bees—and poisonous plants. It's also good for treating cuts and scrapes.
- **Tea tree (*Melaleuca alternifolia*):** Tea tree oil reduces histamine-induced (allergic) inflammation of the skin and can decrease the welt left from insect bites and stings. It also has antibacterial properties to help prevent infection.
- **Witch-hazel (*Hamamelis virginiana*):** A powerful astringent, witch-hazel can dry up "weeping" rashes and create a virtual bandage over the area by sealing cell membranes and reducing the permeability of surrounding

blood vessels. Research shows it performs better than hydrogen peroxide in helping skin heal. It's also a strong antimicrobial and antioxidant.

## Creating Insect Repellents

Several popular culinary herbs and spices contain chemicals with serious bug-repellent abilities. Recent studies have shown that extracts of cinnamon (*Cinnamomum verum, C. aromaticum*), clove (*Syzygium aromaticum*), fennel (*Foeniculum vulgare*), and ginger (*Zingiber officinale*) can keep mosquitoes, ticks, and other insects away.

### HERBAL REMEDIES FOR REPELLING INSECTS

Other herbal alternatives to chemical repellents include:

- **Camphor (*Cinnamomum camphora*):** Camphor (the herb) contains camphor (the chemical), which is a natural insect repellent. It's also an effective pain and itch reliever (approved by the Food and Drug Administration), so you can use it to treat bites you've already got.
- **Lemon eucalyptus (*Eucalyptus citriodora, Corymbia citriodora*):** The oil from this Australian native is registered with the FDA and was recently approved as an insect repellent by the Centers for Disease Control and Prevention.

- **Neem (*Azadirachta indica*)**: Topical neem preparations have been shown to repel several species of mosquitoes.

## Battling the Cold and Flu

Unfortunately, everyone is familiar with colds and the flu. The sniffling, coughing, and aching muscles are symptoms you've likely experienced more than a few times. However, you can prevent falling victim to the next circulating bug by boosting your immune system with healthy foods. Most people treat colds and flu with over-the-counter pain relievers, decongestants, antihistamines, and cough medicines. These drugs can cause a long list of side effects, including irregular heartbeat, drowsiness, and stomach pain. Fortunately, there are natural remedies you can use to get healthy without harming your body with chemicals.

Beta-carotene plays a role in the function of the skin and mucous membranes that line the nose and lungs. This is your body's first defense against invading germs that could cause a cold or the flu. Beta-carotene also increases the presence of T cells, which attack invaders that can make you sick.

### HERBAL REMEDIES FOR COLDS

The following herbal remedies will help you with cold and flu symptoms:

- **Andrographis (*Andrographis paniculata*):** Andrographis is used in Ayurvedic and Chinese medicine to treat upper respiratory tract infections (it's an antibacterial and antioxidant). Studies show it can relieve the symptoms of sore throats and help prevent colds.
- **Astragalus (*Astragalus membranaceus*):** Astragalus is used in traditional Chinese medicine as a tonic for the immune system. Studies show it's an antiviral, antibacterial, and immunomodulator that helps prevent infections.
- **Echinacea (*Echinacea purpurea*):** Echinacea is a powerful antiviral and immune system stimulant that's been shown in several studies to reduce the severity and duration of cold and flu symptoms.
- **Elderberry (*Sambucus nigra*):** Elderberry has both antiviral and immune-boosting effects, making it a great remedy for colds and flu. Research shows it can fight several viruses at once and improve your symptoms in just a few days.
- **Ginger (*Zingiber officinale*):** Ginger inhibits the bacteria and viruses responsible for upper respiratory infections and also relieves sore throats and the aches of the flu.
- **Isatis (*Isatis tinctoria*):** Constituents of this Chinese herb have antiviral, antibacterial, antifungal, analgesic, and antipyretic (fever-reducing) capabilities.

## CINNAMON-ECHINACEA COLD SYRUP RECIPE

This herbal cold syrup is perfect for treating colds and flu—especially in kids. Remember to not give honey to children younger than a year old.

**You will need:**

- 1 part cinnamon (*Cinnamomum verum, C. aromaticum*) bark
- 1 part dried echinacea (*Echinacea purpurea*) root
- ½ part fresh ginger (*Zingiber officinalis*) root, grated or chopped
- 1 cup honey (or sweetener of your choice)

**Directions**

1. Add 2 ounces (about 8 tablespoons) of the herb mixture to a quart of cold water in a large stockpot. Place on the stove and bring to a boil, then simmer until the liquid is reduced by half (leave the lid slightly ajar).
2. Strain the herbs from the liquid and discard, then pour the liquid back into the pot.
3. Add 1 cup honey (or other sweetener) and heat the mixture through.
4. Remove from heat, let cool, and transfer to glass bottles. Store in the refrigerator.

# Relieving Headaches

A headache is classified as any pain in the head, neck, or scalp area. The most common types are those associated with tension resulting from stress, anxiety, or depression. Headaches can also occur due to overexertion or improper alignment when sitting at a desk or while sleeping, and sinus headaches often accompany a sinus infection or cold. Migraine headaches are much more severe; they include nausea and can affect vision, such as causing light flashes during the "aura" period preceding or during a headache.

Low levels of the mineral magnesium have been linked to headaches. Magnesium has many functions in the body, including reducing pain and calming the central nervous system, thus reducing stress levels. It is involved in the regulation and production of the brain chemical serotonin and helps regulate blood sugar levels. Current research suggests that rapid drops in blood sugar may be one trigger for migraine sufferers. Some studies have also found a link between increased riboflavin, a B vitamin, and decreased migraine headaches.

## HERBAL REMEDIES FOR HEADACHES

Many traditional herbal formulas have shown the ability to handle even the toughest headaches:

- **Butterbur (*Petasites hybridus*):** Extracts from this shrub have analgesic, anti-inflammatory, and antiseizure actions. In several recent studies, they produced a marked decrease in the severity and frequency of migraines.

- **Cayenne (*Capsicum annuum, C. frutescens*):** Applied topically, cayenne preparations have been shown to relieve and even prevent the devastating pain of cluster headaches.
- **Feverfew (*Tanacetum parthenium*):** This is perhaps the best-known herbal headache remedy. It has been shown in several studies to reduce the frequency of migraine attacks and limit their symptoms when they do occur.
- **Lavender (*Lavandula angustifolia*):** The essential oil of this flowering plant has been used effectively to treat several types of headache pain. The same is true of peppermint oil (*Mentha × piperita*).
- **Willow (*Salix alba*):** The salicin from the bark of this tree is a potent analgesic. Its headache-fighting properties are well proven in both laboratory and clinical studies.

HEADACHE RELIEF TINCTURE RECIPE

Keep the following relaxing, pain-fighting combination on hand for when headaches strike.

**You will need:**
- 1 part California poppy (*Eschscholzia californica*) seeds
- 1 part feverfew (*Tanacetum parthenium*) leaves and flowers
- 1 part lavender (*Lavandula angustifolia*) flowers

**Directions**

1. Crush the California poppy seeds and finely chop the feverfew and lavender.

2. Put them in a clean glass jar and add enough alcohol—80- or 100-proof vodka, gin, or brandy—to cover them with about 2" or 3" of fluid.

3. Cover with a tight-fitting lid, place in a warm, dark spot, and leave it there for four to six weeks—the longer, the better.

4. Once a day, shake the jar to keep the herbs from settling at the bottom.

5. When the time is up, strain the herbs and discard them. Transfer the tincture to a small glass bottle (ideally one with a dropper to make it easier to get the right dose). Stored properly, it will keep for two years or longer. Be sure to keep tinctures out of the reach of children.

## Dealing with Insomnia

According to the Mayo Clinic, insomnia is one of the most common medical complaints. Fortunately, there are many foods that have calming effects that can improve your ability to sleep well and wake feeling rested. A recent nationwide survey found that one in five Americans takes a prescription or over-the-counter sleep aid at least once a week—and 63 percent of them experience side effects.

*Insomnia can be triggered by several medications, including cold and allergy medications (antihistamines and decongestants), hypertension and heart disease drugs, birth control pills, thyroid medicines, and asthma medications. Caffeine is an obvious cause for insomnia but it's found in many places beyond your coffee cup, including some over-the-counter pain relievers.*

Insomnia can be caused by a variety of factors. Stress and anxiety may trigger it, or it may result from a separate medical condition or current medication. Caffeine and alcohol can cause insomnia, as can eating late at night.

According to the National Sleep Foundation, the amino acid tryptophan can cause sleepiness. Through a series of chemical reactions, tryptophan raises levels of serotonin in the brain, which helps regulate sleep patterns. Carbohydrates can help make you sleepy because they make tryptophan more available for the brain to use.

## HERBAL REMEDIES FOR INSOMNIA

Here are some useful herbal remedies if you're not getting the sleep you need:

- **Chamomile (*Matricaria recutita*):** Chamomile flowers have been used to make bedtime teas for centuries. They contain mildly sedating compounds as well as chemicals that reduce anxiety.

- **Kava (*Piper methysticum*):** Research shows this herb can be as effective as the drug Valium in creating the changes in brain waves that help you fall—and stay—asleep.
- **Lavender (*Lavandula angustifolia*):** Lavender oil is used topically as a sedative and antianxiety agent. Research shows it can promote relaxation and induce sleep in people of all ages. In one study, people who used lavender in aromatherapy (they inhaled it or applied it to their skin) before going to bed reported feeling more refreshed in the morning.
- **Lemon balm (*Melissa officinalis*):** Lemon balm is a mild sedative and stress reliever. Research shows it can quell anxiety and promote sleep.
- **Passionflower (*Passiflora incarnata*):** Passionflower is a mild sedative and sleep aid.
- **Valerian (*Valeriana officinalis*):** Valerian is a mild sedative and tranquilizer. Studies show its chemical compounds can have a direct effect on gamma-aminobutyric acid (GABA), a brain chemical that controls arousal and sleep. Taking valerian can shorten the time it takes you to fall asleep (sleep latency) and improve your quality of sleep.

## ANTI-INSOMNIA TEA RECIPE

Try the following herbal tea when you're suffering from sleepless nights.

**You will need:**
- 2 parts chamomile (*Matricaria recutita*) flowers
- 2 parts passionflower (*Passiflora incarnata*) leaves and flowers
- 2 parts lemon balm (*Melissa officinalis*) leaves
- 1 part valerian (*Valeriana officinalis*) root
- ½ part rose (*Rosa canina, R. spp.*) hips (the round portion of the flower just below the petals)
- ¼ part lavender (*Lavandula angustifolia*) flowers

**Directions**
1. Put all the ingredients into a tea strainer and place the strainer over a mug.
2. Fill the mug with boiling water. Use about 1 teaspoon of dried herbs per mug of water.
3. Cover the mug; the medicinal value of many herbs is contained in their essential oils, so you'll want to keep the steam from escaping.
4. Steep 15 minutes or longer. The longer you let it steep, the stronger your tea will be.
5. Drink in the evening, at least an hour or two before bed (you don't want to wake up because you need to use the bathroom). If you want something stronger, you can make this formula into a tincture, taking ¼ teaspoon of the tincture at bedtime.

# Treating Muscle Cramps

As you move, you contract and relax your muscles. When a muscle involuntarily contracts, that's called a spasm. When the spasm lasts a long time and the muscle can't relax, it becomes a cramp. A muscle cramp can last anywhere from a few minutes to an entire day.

Cramps are most often caused by a nerve malfunction and many occur after physical activity or during the night. Dehydration and reduced mineral intake are two dietary causes of the malfunction that can result in a cramp.

Other causes of cramps include:

- Heavy exercising (or exercising for too long)
- Electrolyte imbalances
- Muscle fatigue
- Lack of calcium or potassium

Adequate intake of the electrolytes potassium, sodium, magnesium, and calcium can reduce the risk of cramps due to the role these minerals play in hydration and muscle action. Maintaining a healthy balance of these minerals in the body reduces the risk of muscle cramps.

## HEALING WITH HERBS

To fight the pain of most muscle injuries, try these herbal remedies:

- **Arnica (*Arnica montana*):** Arnica is a classic remedy for all types of aches, including the sports-induced kind. Studies have confirmed its use as a remedy for soft-tissue (i.e., muscle) injuries.
- **Cayenne (*Capsicum annuum, C. frutescens*):** These peppers contain a chemical called capsaicin that can be applied topically to produce a warming sensation and reduce pain (it's the key ingredient in many over-the-counter muscle rubs).
- **Comfrey (*Symphytum officinale*):** This herb is used topically to treat all kinds of sports injuries, including injuries to muscles, tendons, and ligaments.
- **Eucalyptus (*Eucalyptus globulus*):** The oil from this Australian plant is used topically as an analgesic and anesthetic.
- **Peppermint (*Mentha × piperita*):** Peppermint contains menthol, a natural anesthetic and painkiller. Menthol also produces a soothing, cooling sensation.
- **Pineapple (*Ananas comosus*):** Pineapple's active constituent, bromelain, can be taken internally to treat a variety of sports injuries and trauma. Studies have shown it can reduce inflammation, swelling, and bruising.
- **Saint John's wort (*Hypericum perforatum*):** This herb produces an oil that's used topically to treat muscle and joint injuries (it has analgesic, anti-edema, and anesthetic constituents). It also works as an anti-inflammatory and antispasmodic.

- **Yarrow (*Achillea millefolium*):** Yarrow relieves pain and swelling and is a classic remedy for bruising and muscle soreness.

## Managing Stress and Anxiety

Stress is a natural part of life, and that's not necessarily a bad thing. It's often psychological stress that gets you out of bed in the morning or to the gym in the evening. It's what makes you perform well at the office or in the classroom and do basically everything you need to survive. Unfortunately, too much stress—problems that go on for too long or demand too much of your resources—can wreak havoc on your health. Chronic, unresolved stress has been linked to a host of diseases, including cardiovascular disease and cancer. It's also been tied to many mental disorders, such as depression.

According to the National Institutes of Health, low levels of vitamin $B_{12}$ can contribute to feelings of stress and anxiety. Other vitamins play a role in the production and function of neurotransmitters, some of which affect mood, relaxation, and emotions. These include vitamins C, $B_6$, $B_1$, $B_2$, and folate. In addition, the amino acid tryptophan influences the production of serotonin in the brain, which has a calming effect. Low levels of magnesium are also linked to increased and chronic anxiety.

## HERBAL REMEDIES FOR STRESS

Try these anxiety-busting herbs:

- **Ashwagandha (*Withania somnifera*):** Ashwagandha is an Ayurvedic remedy for stress-related anxiety and insomnia. Studies show it inhibits the release of stress hormones and calms the central nervous system.
- **Asian ginseng (*Panax ginseng*):** Asian ginseng is one of the best-researched herbs around and has been used for centuries to help people manage stress. Recent research has shown it can protect the brain from damage caused by chronic stress.
- **Ginkgo (*Ginkgo biloba*):** Ginkgo is famous for its brain-boosting powers. In the lab, it's shown an ability to offset many effects of stress, such as memory deficits and depression.
- **Lavender (*Lavandula angustifolia*):** The essential oil of this fragrant plant has proven antianxiety properties when applied topically or inhaled. In laboratory tests, it performed as well as the drug Valium.
- **Lemon balm (*Melissa officinalis*):** This herb relieves stress and induces relaxation. Research shows it can improve your mood, increase your alertness (and mental processing speeds), and produce a general feeling of well-being.
- **Saint John's wort (*Hypericum perforatum*):** This herb has been shown to alleviate cognitive effects of stress, such as

lapses in working memory, as well as the decreased physical performance and feelings of anxiety that stress can produce.

- **Schisandra (*Schisandra chinensis*):** This herb balances your nervous and endocrine (hormone) systems and is particularly good at helping you manage psychological stress. Research shows it can increase your mental performance and adjust the levels of the stress hormone cortisol in your system.

## CALMING MASSAGE OIL RECIPE

Make this oil with soothing lavender to calm your nerves after a long day. This infusion contains three tried-and-true herbal relaxants, plus three moisturizing plant oils.

**You will need:**
- 1 part coconut (*Cocos nucifera*) oil
- 1 part almond (*Prunus dulcis*) oil
- 1 part cocoa (*Theobroma cacao*) butter
- 1 part chamomile (*Matricaria recutita*) flowers
- 1 part lavender (*Lavandula angustifolia*) leaves
- 1 part lemon balm (*Melissa officinalis*) leaves and flowers

## Directions

1. Put all the ingredients into the top section of a double boiler, then fill the bottom section with water and bring it to a low boil.
2. Let the oil simmer gently 30–60 minutes, checking frequently to make sure the oil isn't overheating (it will start to smoke if that's the case).
3. Strain the oil and allow to cool before use.

CHAPTER 5

# CANDLE MAKING

The art of making candles is not only a relaxing and creative endeavor but also one that provides you with a product that is both useful and beautiful. The warm scent of wax, the slow pouring or rolling of the candle, the satisfaction of lighting and using your final project—candle making is a calming way to work with your hands. This chapter will discuss the types of candles you can make and take you step-by-step through making several types of rolled and poured candles. Soon you'll have candles to light your home or to give as homemade gifts to friends and family!

## Types of Candles

Before you delve into candle making, it will be useful to have a background in the different types of candles available. The kind of candle you'll want to make will differ depending on your need—for example, the candle you'd craft as the centerpiece for a dinner party is very different from the candles you may keep on hand in case of a blackout.

Here are some of the more common types of candles:

- **Container**—A container candle is poured into a mold and sets in the shape of that mold.
- **Pillar**—A popular candle shape, the pillar is a thick candle (usually 3"-4" in diameter). Most pillars are cylindrical but they can be made in any shape—oval, hexagonal, square, and so on. Commercial pillar candles come in standard sizes (such as 3" × 6") but you can make one in any size you choose.
- **Tapers**—Tapered candles are what most people think of first when they think "candle." The most common candle shape—often found on dinner tables during festivities—tapers are expressly made to fit into a candleholder of some sort, whether for a single candle or multiple candles.
- **Tealight**—Tealights are similar to votives but are smaller, flatter cylinders usually only ½" high and 1½" in diameter.
- **Votive**—The term *votive* comes from the Latin for "to vow"; votive candles were originally used in churches to light the front of an icon or a sculpture of a saint while asking for intercession. In recent years, this type of candle has become very popular for home use as well, especially as scented candles of different colors. Votives are usually cylinders that are 2"-3" high and about 1½" in diameter.

# Choosing Your Wax

When most people think of making a candle, the first thing that comes to mind is wax. Wax, put simply, is what your candle burns for fuel. As the wick burns, the candle wax melts and is wicked into the flame to feed its fire. Although in times past candles were made of tallow (animal fat), those days are long gone. Nowadays you will likely rely on wax or wax with additives for your home candle making. Most candles today are made of beeswax, paraffin, or a combination of the two.

### BEESWAX

Beeswax is the most elegant of the waxes available for candle making. Just as silkworms are famous for making fine silk, bees make excellent wax. Beeswax, because it is permeated with honey during its preharvest life, naturally has a wonderful, sweet fragrance. Its odor will vary depending on what the bees are feeding on, which might be wildflowers, clover, avocados, or various herbs. Unrefined beeswax in its natural state has a golden yellow to brownish or reddish-brown color. It also contains plant parts and bits of the bees themselves.

Harvesting and purifying beeswax is a time-consuming, difficult process, so it's not surprising that beeswax is far more expensive than paraffin. However, one of its advantages is that it's long lasting. Beeswax is also very lovely when it burns; it creates a warm, golden glow that nothing else can match, and the sweet honeyed smell permeates the house and people's hair and clothes. However, for budgetary purposes, beeswax can be combined with paraffin to make candles that will be long-lasting yet less expensive.

Sheets of beeswax were originally invented by beekeepers. These were, and still are, used to line beehives. This wax liner gives bees a firm foundation on which to build their honeycombs, thus beekeepers call beeswax sheets "brood foundation." Beeswax candles can be made from foundation sheets. If you've followed the beekeeping advice in Chapter 1, you might obtain beeswax this way.

### PARAFFIN

Since pure beeswax is a rare commodity and quite expensive, most beeswax candles you'll find today are mixed with paraffin, a byproduct of the refining process that turns crude oil into motor oil.

Paraffin waxes used for candle making are classified by their melting points: low, medium, and high. In general, most homemade candles need to melt at 125°F–150°F. Never buy grocery store paraffin for candle making—it is not the same as the paraffin wax used to make candles. It has a lower melting point and doesn't harden sufficiently to make a candle stand up straight.

Stearin, or stearic acid, is added to paraffin to make it harder and to increase opacity. Some paraffin wax comes with stearin already mixed in, usually 10 percent. Alternatively, you can buy stearin separately and mix it into the paraffin to suit your needs.

Although it is possible to make candles from paraffin wax alone, there are definite advantages to adding stearin to paraffin, including:

- Stearin makes candles easier to remove from their molds because they contract more during the cooling process.
- Candles made with stearin have a longer burn time.
- Paraffin is translucent and can make for a dull-looking candle. Adding stearin makes the candle opaque and much whiter, giving it a nicer appearance.

If you're using stearin, check the label on the package. The supplier's information will make clear exactly how to use it and in what proportion.

You can buy paraffin wax in pellets or powdered form, both of which are easier to measure or weigh and handle. However, bulk is cheaper. Bulk paraffin is normally sold by suppliers and craft shops in 11-pound slabs; the next standard size up is a 55-pound case. The best way to break up the 11-pound slabs is to put one into a heavy-duty disposable trash bag and drop it from shoulder height to the floor.

## RECYCLED WAX

You can save money and help protect the environment by recycling old wax, including cheese coverings, crayons, and sealing wax. Save all your candle ends, as well as any scraps left over from making candles, and store them either in zippered plastic bags (away from heat) or in an airtight tin such as the type in which Christmas cookies are sold. You can also chip, scrape, or melt the dregs of votive cups and save them too. And, of course, any failed homemade candles with which you weren't satisfied can be reused to make new, (hopefully) successful candles.

You can remelt everything (keeping colors separate, if necessary). Strain melted candle ends through a fine sieve or cheesecloth to remove burned bits. Use a hammer to break up large chunks of recycled wax into smaller pieces for remelting. Be sure to save all the wax that gets spilled during your candle making efforts—a putty knife is a good tool for scraping up spills.

Keep in mind when using colorful wax that some shades lend themselves to reuse more easily than others. Pink can be turned to rose or red, lavender or purple. On the other hand, 5 pounds of blazingly bright magenta isn't what you'd call versatile. Of course, if your leftover wax is white, you're home free.

 *Red seems to be the most powerful of dyes, yet it can be overwhelming. Recycled blends of wax (candle ends, leftovers) with colors that have red in them will ordinarily turn out with a reddish cast, even if red isn't the largest proportion of color in your mixture.*

You can separate your candle scraps by color if you like, or throw the whole bunch in together—if you're in the mood to experiment, melting different candle colors together can be the way to go. A yellow cheese coating mixed with a green scented candle might give you a nice lime color.

## Types of Wicks

If the first component of a candle is wax, it follows that the next is the wick. Indeed, the wick is the heart of the candle, not only in that it lies at the center but also in that it's what determines if a candle will burn and how well.

Modern wicks are a braided or cored bunch of threads, usually made of cotton but sometimes of linen or other fabric. The material is then subjected to a process known as mordanting, where it's pickled in a chemical solution intended to make it fire-retardant.

Candle making suppliers sell packaged wicks to people looking to make their own candles. These prepackaged wicks are ordinarily classified by the diameter of the candle with which they should be used, for example:

- Extra small = 0"–1"
- Small = 1"–2"
- Large = 2"–3"
- Extra large = 4" or greater

There are two basic kinds of modern wicks: cored and braided. Cored wicks are woven around a central core made up of paper, cotton, zinc, or lead. This helps them stand upright. Braided wicks come in either a flat or square-braided type, both in a full range of sizes. The flat-braided type is just like a braid of hair: a three-strand braid made of many tiny threads. Flat-braided wicks are sized according to the number of these small threads, called plies, in each wick. Square-braided wicks look like square columns with rounded corners. They are available in various sizes and are classified according to different numbering systems.

## Priming Your Wick

Prior to use, all wicks need to be primed. This is a process that saturates the wick with wax in advance of it being placed in the candle mold or dipped. Priming is done to eliminate air that may have become trapped in the plies of the braid.

Usually, when you pour the wax over the wick or dip the wick, air is forced out naturally. However, this can't be relied on, so it's best to prime the wick before use. This is especially important for the poured container candles you'll learn to make later in this chapter.

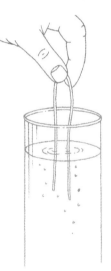

To prime a wick, follow these steps:

1. Heat your wax to 160°F (using a thermometer to check the temperature).
2. Dip the length of wick into the wax. Air bubbles will form as the air escapes. Continue to hold the wick in the wax until you no longer see air bubbles (usually about 5 minutes).

**Figure 5-1:**
*Priming the wick*

3. Once the wax stops bubbling, remove the wick from the pot of wax and stretch it out. Allow it to cool thoroughly.
4. When completely dry, the wick should be stiff. At this point, it's ready to use.

Always trim the wick to within ½" of the wax surface before lighting the candle. For larger candles, especially pillars, allow the candle to burn for at least 2 hours before extinguishing to distribute the liquid wax evenly. Don't burn large-diameter candles for longer than 3 hours at a time, otherwise you risk destabilizing the candle.

## Equipment You'll Need

In addition to wax and wicks, making candles at home requires some basic equipment, most of which is neither expensive nor complicated. You probably already have most of these essentials in your kitchen or home.

*If you choose to use any of your cooking implements and/or pots for making candles at home, dedicate any and all of that equipment to candle making only. Not only will you avoid confusion, you'll also keep your food safe from contamination from wax, additives, dyes, and the like.*

## THERMOMETER

You can buy a special wax thermometer or use a candy or other cooking thermometer that covers a scale from 0°F–300°F. It should have a clip so you can immerse it deep enough into your pot of melting wax to get an accurate reading. And make sure your thermometer is accurate. You must always know the precise degree to which your wax has been heated. Check your thermometer regularly and discontinue use if it's no longer accurate.

## DOUBLE BOILERS

Obviously, a system for melting wax is the primary consideration in candle making. For the novice candlemaker, the best melting method is using a double boiler. Double boilers are extremely easy to improvise. You only need an outer pot to hold water and an inner pot in which to melt the wax. The outer pot must be large enough to hold an amount of water sufficient to rise two-thirds of the way up the exterior of the inner pot.

For the poured candles in this book, you can use a shallow round pot, big enough to melt as much wax as you'll need. You can put one saucepan over another or rest a fireproof bowl on a saucepan (though your wax may melt unevenly). Ideally, the inner pot will have a handle (a metal pitcher is excellent). A large can, such as the kind fruit juice is sold in, will work if you're willing to ladle out the wax. You can pour from such a can if you use mitts to protect your hands from the heat and are very careful.

If you improvise your double boiler, you'll need a support for the inner pot, such as a metal trivet (the kind used on a dinner table to protect it from a hot dish). A support can be improvised as well, for instance by using three short cans (tuna fish or cat food cans will do). Cut out both ends and wire them together to make a three-pointed support, or cut out one end only and fill them with water so they don't float.

 *Never put your wax-melting container directly on the heat source, and keep a careful watch on the water level in your outer pot. Never let it boil dry. Add water frequently while melting wax.*

You can also buy ready-made double boilers in many sizes. Cast aluminum and stainless steel double boilers for cooking are readily available wherever cookware is sold.

Whichever kind of double boiler you use, you'll need to replenish the water in the bottom pot frequently to keep your boiling water at the correct level. Your working surface must be level and have ready access to a water supply. You also need a heat source that isn't an open flame. Your electric stove will work fine and a steady hot plate will suffice as well. Clean your melting vessel with paper towels after each use.

## MISCELLANEOUS EQUIPMENT

Depending on what kind of candle you make and which method you use, there are a few other necessary supplies. These ancillary but vital items are listed more or less in order of importance, though all will prove useful as you continue to expand your efforts. And this list isn't necessarily all-inclusive—you may think of other tools or implements that will be useful as you become more experienced.

### Cake Pans and Cookie Sheets

Cake pans and cookie sheets are multipurpose. You can line them with nonstick pan spray or vegetable oil and pour on unused melted wax to cool. They are also useful as pads for containers of hot wax.

### Scale

A scale is an important piece of equipment you can't do without. Chances are you already have a kitchen scale that will do. It should have a range of 0–10 pounds measured in ounces. You can also use a gram scale but you'll need to convert between grams and ounces and pounds. A scale is necessary for weighing not only wax but also additives such as stearic acid.

### Pyrex Measuring Cups

Pyrex measuring cups come in 1-, 2-, 4-, and 6-cup sizes and are heat resistant. You can use the cups to determine the volume of wax by displacement. Put wax in one cup in a block or chunks, then put water in the second cup and note the amount it takes to fully submerge the wax in the first cup. Subtract the volume of water added from the level of water needed to cover the wax. The result is the volume of wax you've just measured.

Since Pyrex measuring cups can be heated, you can also use them (or any heatproof calibrated vessel, such as a chemistry flask) as a wax melting insert when melting small amounts of wax in an improvised double boiler.

### Oven Mitts and Potholders

Oven mitts or potholders are essential when it comes to protecting your hands when handling a pot of hot wax.

### Metal Ruler or Straightedge

It's a good idea to have an artist's T-square and a heavy metal ruler. These are useful for cutting and calibrating lengths of vessels, candles, and wicks. These tools are available at art supply shops, which often also sell craft materials. You can use the straightedge to cut sheet wax for the rolled candles you'll learn about later in this chapter.

### Cutting Surface

A cutting surface can be a laminated kitchen counter that can't be cut-marked or a wooden or plastic cutting board such as those used for chopping food. You can even use a piece of heavy cardboard.

### Cutting Tools

For cutting tools, X-Acto knives work well. The blades are extremely sharp and run cleanly along a straight edge. Your cutting tool is for cutting sheets of wax for rolled and stacked candles and for trimming the seams of finished molded candles. Scissors are also useful, especially for cutting wicks.

### Stirrers

If you're adding stearin to paraffin wax, you'll need to mix it in as it's melting. Practically any old thing will do for stirring the melted wax but old long-handled wooden spoons are ideal. If you don't have any, chances are you can pick up some inexpensive ones at a garage or yard sale or at a flea market.

You can get a paint stirrer for free at your local paint store. Paint stirrers are flat paddles given away with the purchase of paint, and paint store salespeople are usually happy to give you a few extra because they're imprinted with advertising for the brand of paint and/or the store. When you have an occasion to buy paint, ask for extra stirrers and stash them away.

### Ladle

You might also need a ladle. Choose one impervious to heat with a deep bowl and a comfortably angled handle to avoid spilling.

### Greaseproof Paper and Paper Towels

Greaseproof papers include waxed paper, parchment, brown craft paper (or brown paper bags flattened out), and foil. Keep a good supply on hand to cover work surfaces. And don't forget rags or paper towels—they're essential for cleanups, to use as oil wipes, to mop up water spills, and for many other chores.

### Dowels

When making the container candles later in this chapter, you'll need a straight rod of some kind to tie the wick to while you pour wax around it. Your dowel can be a chopstick or a piece of cardboard, anything that will support the weight of the wick.

### Wick Sustainers

These are little metal disks that are used to anchor the wick in container candles, votives, and tealights. Wick sustainers are available wherever candle making supplies are sold. To use, push the wick through a small hole in the sustainer and pinch the metal together so it sits flat on the container base.

### Paint Scraper

A paint scraper is excellent for easily scraping spilled wax off a hard surface, such as a counter. You might also use a putty knife.

### Weights

Small weights with a center hole are required to weigh down wicks. Washers, curtain weights, and nuts will all do.

## Safety Tips to Keep In Mind

Before you begin to work with wax, it must be heated to its particular melting point. Take care not to overheat your wax. The burning point of wax is the temperature at which the properties of a particular wax have been stretched beyond the safety mark.

For example, paraffin should not usually be heated to more than 200°F. Never leave melting wax on the heat source unattended—it is as volatile as cooking oil and can catch fire if overheated. Always keep a large pot lid handy to smother a fire should one start. Keep damp cloths handy for the same purpose.

Waxes are highly flammable (that's why candles burn!) and can catch fire. The temperature at which they combust is the flash point. This is approximately 440°F, depending on the type of wax you use. Never heat wax to the flash point. Watch your thermometer carefully. If your wax does catch fire, stay calm and do the following:

- Turn off the heat immediately. Don't move the pan.
- Smother flames with a metal lid or damp towel.
- Never use water to put out a wax fire.

It is also smart to have an ABC-type fire extinguisher on hand as well as baking soda (dumped into a fire it will smother the flames immediately).

*Always remember that the wax you are pouring is hot and it can burn you if spilled on your skin. Don't pour when you're distracted or feeling jittery. Teach yourself to pour in a smooth, steady stream by practicing with water, using the vessel in which you plan to melt the wax.*

## Cleaning Up

Always cover your work surface with disposable paper. Don't use old newspapers to cover working surfaces as the newsprint may transfer to the undersurface if wax spills on it. Use brown wrapping paper or tin foil (use foil on your stove) to facilitate cleanup. Or, if you can devote an entire countertop to candle making, get a laminated one with a smooth surface from which you can easily scrape up cooled wax.

After each candle making session, be sure to clean up your workspace, especially if it's in your kitchen. Then you won't have to clean up before you start another session. Gather all your tools and materials (knives, scrapers, wicks, colorants, scent bottles, and so on), wipe off or scrape any waxy residue, and store them in the place you regularly keep them. Always keep rags and paper towels handy. Use them to wipe any waxy surfaces while they're still warm. After you've cleaned up all the waxy containers and surfaces, dispose of the paper towels or rags. Do not incinerate them.

Never pour liquid wax down your drain. It will solidify and cause a severe blockage, not to mention a huge plumbing bill. Also, don't pour your hot double boiler water down your drain. It may have wax in it, unbeknownst to you. Dispose of the water outside or let it cool until the wax hardens, then remove the wax before pouring the water down the drain.

Pour leftover melted wax into muffin tins or other small cups. Once it's cooled you can pop out the hardened wax and store it in plastic bags for future use. Don't throw away your leftovers, even the small scraps, including candle ends or the bottoms of container candles. Wax costs money, and recycling saves both money and work.

## Handmade Rolled Candles

Rolled candles are made from sheets of wax and, as the name implies, the wax is rolled around a wick, much as you would roll a sheet of dough around a filling to make jelly rolls. This is the simplest method of making candles. It's easiest for the beginner and is a good introduction to the world of candle making.

Wax sheets specially made for rolling are available at craft shops and from candle making suppliers and come in dozens of lovely colors (although, later in this chapter, you will learn how to make your own).

There are two types of commercially prepared wax sheets for making rolled candles. The majority are made of pure beeswax, which, although more expensive, is longer burning than paraffin or paraffin with stearic acid. The second type of sheet wax is a mixture of beeswax and paraffin, which is less expensive than pure beeswax. Also available, though in shorter supply, are sheets of paraffin without beeswax. These are the least expensive of all but have the disadvantage of a much shorter burn time.

Most wax sheets for rolled candles are formed in a honeycomb pattern. This type of sheet is embossed with a hexagonal indentation—it looks like the wax from a honeycomb. The most common size is 8" × 16" but you can cut the sheets to suit your specific purpose. The honeycomb-patterned sheets are rolled out under an embossing wheel. Sheets can be purchased in natural beeswax colors (pale honey to dark brown) or in various colors that have been added as dyes after the wax was bleached.

Another type of wax for making rolled candles is smooth and flat. These are useful when you don't want a textured candle. The pure-white smooth sheets make an elegant-looking candle that gives a stylish appearance.

## KEEPING YOUR SHEETS WARM

Sheets of beeswax bought preformed in a honeycomb pattern are ready for use. However, they need to be warm enough to be pliable before you start to roll. A blow-dryer is a handy tool to keep on hand for warming sheets of wax. Beeswax is the easiest to work with because of its natural flexibility.

Paraffin or beeswax/paraffin blend wax sheets are used in the same manner but paraffin tends to be brittle. Therefore, a blend or straight paraffin will be a bit more difficult to handle, requiring extra attention to keep the sheets warm enough to be pliable. If your wax sheets have cooled and aren't pliable enough to roll, you can do several things:

- Using your blow-dryer, waft warm air over the sheets of wax.
- Iron them between sheets of paper with a warm iron.
- Quickly dip the sheets into hot water.

## MAKING YOUR OWN WAX SHEETS

Although using purchased wax sheets is the easiest way to make rolled candles, if you're adventuresome—and if you have some leftover wax you want to use—you can make your own wax sheets.

**You will need:**
- A piece of plywood the size of the sheet you want
- Wax
- A large, deep pot for melting the wax (a deep steamer of the type used for asparagus or corn will work, as will a deep stockpot)

**Directions**
1. To prepare the plywood, soak it in water for 1 hour or more (to prevent it from absorbing the hot wax).
2. Melt your wax in the pot.
3. Dip the plywood into the melted wax, using tongs or pliers to hold it firmly. Allow the wax-covered plywood to cool for about a minute.
4. Dip the wax-covered board into the wax again, and again allow it to cool.
5. Repeat this process five or more times depending on the thickness of the wax sheet you want.
6. Scrape the wax at the edges of the board, then peel off the sheet.

Homemade wax sheets lend themselves to various uses. Although purchased sheets come in various colors, you can tint your own wax sheets any color you like or make multicolored layers for an interesting effect.

What's nice about homemade sheet wax is you don't have to warm it up before using it; it will be warm when you remove it from the board. While it's still warm, you can form it into different shapes as you roll it.

Should the wax cool too much, just drop it into hot water (100°F–110°F) for a minute or two to soften it again. Keep a pot of warm water handy for this purpose.

## PREPARING THE WICK

Pick your wicks based on what you plan for the diameter of your finished rolled candles. There is no need to prime (prewax) the entire wick to make a rolled candle; however, the tip of the wick needs to be primed prior to being lit. To do this, simply pull a small corner piece of wax from the edge of the sheet and press it around the end of the wick.

## ROLLING YOUR CANDLE

You can make rolled candles any diameter you like. You can make tall, slender rolled candles with two or three sheets. Medium- and large-sized rolled candles can be made simply by adding more sheets until you reach the size you prefer. Rolled candles lend themselves to various shapes, the most common and easiest being a simple cylinder. To make this type of rolled candle, lay out the sheet (preferably on a warm surface) and lay on it a wick cut to the proper size. Begin rolling at the short end of the sheet and keep rolling until you reach the other end.

**You will need:**

- A hard cutting surface
- Wick (or wicks if you plan to make several candles); use a flat-braided wick for beeswax and a square-braided wick for paraffin
- Scissors (for cutting the wick)
- Sheets of wax made for rolling (either store-bought or homemade)
- A blow-dryer or warming tray
- A sharp knife or razor blade
- A straightedge or ruler

**Directions**

1. Make sure your cutting surface is properly prepared. It should be covered with a piece of heavy cardboard or a mat.
2. Decide what size rolled candle you want to make. Cut a wick (or wicks) 2" longer than the size of the finished candle. Set aside.
3. Warm your wax sheets until they're pliable enough to roll easily. Use a blow-dryer (set on low) or put them on a heating pad or warming tray. Be sure to watch your wax sheets carefully while they're warming. Depending on the warmth of your room, they can easily melt on a heat source. If you accidentally overheat and get a melt, save the wax to make poured candles.

4. Lay the sheet of wax flat on a smooth surface, such as a countertop or table, then bend a ⅛" fold at the end of the short side to make a place for the wick. Press the wick gently into the edge of the wax before beginning to roll. Make sure the wick is firmly embedded in the wax.

5. Next, roll up the wax tightly, making sure the wick is closely held in the wax at each turn. Keep rolling with a firm and even pressure. This prevents air bubbles from forming between the layers. Take care to roll in a straight line to keep the ends flat (for cylindrical candles).

6. When you've rolled the entire sheet, press the final end into the candle so it adheres to the last layer of wax.

7. Once you've finished rolling your candle, cut the wick to ½" in length and neatly trim the bottom end with your knife or razor to get a flat surface on which the candle can rest. If your candle seems uneven or the layers aren't quite close enough, roll the finished candle back and forth on

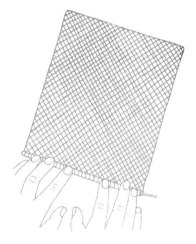

Figure 5-2:
*Rolling a
beeswax candle*

your countertop (like fashioning a roll of cookie dough) until the candle has a round shape and the layers all hold together. Do this with a gentle but firm hand.

*The next time you throw a birthday party, use the rolled method to make homemade birthday candles for the cake!*

## MAKING A ROLLED TAPER

You can carve a taper shape into your rolled candle. To do this, use a sharp knife to trim the wax into a cone shape, then smooth the edges with a heated butter knife. Trim the wick to ½".

*To make sure the bottom of the candle is flat, melt it. Heat up an old metal pan—a pie pan, cake pan, or cookie sheet—over a low flame on the stove and gently press the bottom of the rolled candle onto the metal until it flattens out.*

## MAKING A DIAGONAL ROLLED CANDLE

To make a diagonal rolled candle, cut your sheet of wax in half to make two triangles using your straightedge or ruler and a razor blade or other sharp implement such as an X-Acto knife.

Cut the wick to fit the longer edge and roll the wax sheet toward the pointed end. Take care to keep the long, straight edge even in order to end up with a flat bottom. This method will give you a spiral-shaped candle that is very attractive.

## MAKING A SQUARE-SHAPED ROLLED CANDLE

Using seven sheets of beeswax (9" × 12" each) and a primed wick 10" long, plus 2 ounces of melted beeswax, you can make a square candle. These are quite easy to make with little mess as you need melt only a small amount of wax.

### Directions

1. Lay the primed wick across one beeswax sheet as described in the rolled candle project. Roll up the entire sheet around the wick.

2. Place another sheet of beeswax next to the edge of the end of the first sheet and again roll tightly. Keep the edges even as you roll so they remain the same length.

3. Using your metal ruler, press the sheets against a third sheet of beeswax at a 90-degree angle, pressing the roll into a square shape each time you turn it over.

4. Continue adding the remaining sheets, using the ruler at each turn to make the sides square. After you have the edges shaped, lightly score each remaining sheet against the ruler to help you fold (not roll) the wax around the inner core of squared sheets.

5. Press the end of the final sheet firmly into place as you bend it around the candle. This step will ensure the finished candle doesn't unroll as it burns.

6. Holding the finished candle upside down over a cookie sheet lined with paper to catch the drips, use a small spoon to pour some of the melted beeswax into the cracks between the layers of wax sheets. Smooth some melted wax evenly over the bottom to seal the candle together and give it a flat surface.

## Poured Container Candles

Pouring is the most versatile way to make candles, with a long history dating back far beyond the original pioneers. The first rudimentary lamps were made by pouring oil and wax into containers.

Most of these used some sort of liquid fuel, such as oil or animal fat, that would harden at room temperature, especially in cold climates. In this section, you will learn to make candles that are poured into the containers in which they will be burned.

### CHOOSING A CONTAINER

Container depth is important. Generally speaking, due to the wick's need for adequate oxygen to burn the candle properly, it's a good idea to select containers no more than 5"–6" tall. Shorter ones—even very small ones—are ideal as they burn well and can be made in quantity and set around different areas of a room to give a candlelit feeling to the entire space. For example, baby food jars or other votive candle–sized containers can be utilized this way.

All sorts of food comes in glass jars suitable for making container candles and they often come in interesting shapes. The possibilities are almost endless. Once you become aware of them, you'll notice jars of food that will make excellent and attractive containers, so save them up and you'll have plenty of interesting-looking and original candle containers on hand!

Always pick containers that are either the same diameter at the top and bottom or wide-mouthed at the top. Don't use anything with a narrow neck. Glass and metal are the best materials for containers. Ceramic will also work but is opaque so it will not give a glow as the candle burns down. Never use wood, milk cartons, or any other flammable materials for containers. Glass is a good choice but make sure it's heavy enough not to crack under the burning candle's heat. All sorts of glass containers will work fine. For example, glasses made of heavy recycled glass (usually pale green, made from old Coke bottles) are perfect. Goblets or glasses of heavy glass, often hobnailed (i.e., having bumps on the surface), are very useful and can be refilled indefinitely. Another good choice is the square-shaped heavy glass containers that contain a jelled room deodorizer that evaporates as it's exposed to air. Empty and washed, these types of jars make perfect containers.

*Before you remove the labels from food jars being used to make container candles, make a note of how many ounces the jar holds. You can put the lid on the empty jar with a label marked with the jar's volume. This saves you measuring time.*

Here are some more interesting ideas for unique container candles:

- **Metal ice cube trays** make splendid container candles. Using an ice cube tray has a double advantage. It's easy to pour and you get the effect of a multi-wick candle. When lit, the tray of little cubes gives off a brilliant light.
- **Minimuffin tins** make neat miniature container candles. Line the cups with foil liners before pouring in the wax. When the wax has hardened, lift out each mini-candle. For a dinner party, you can set one of these miniature candles at each person's place, perhaps placed on a saucer.
- **Orange halves.** Slice oranges in half and juice them, then carefully pull out the membrane and pulp until you're down to the shell of the orange peel. Fill with wax. When the wax is cool but not solid, insert a cored wick. These ingenious candles are wonderful for outdoor parties.

## SUPPLIES FOR CONTAINER CANDLES

In addition to the container you've chosen, you'll need the following supplies:

- **Wax:** Usually plain paraffin with a melting point (mp) of 130°F. Remember that the kind of wax you use will influence whether or not you should add stearin. 127 mp wax is sold specifically for use in container candles. It has a soft consistency, low melting point, and holds scent in until the candle is burned, without additives. 128 mp wax is also specially blended for use in containers (and votives) but may require additives. 130 mp does require additives.
- **Stearic acid:** Optional but will give your candle a longer burn time.
- **Wick:** Medium-sized, one for each container; cored wicks are preferable, but not essential. The wick should be 1" longer than the height of the container you're using.
- **Wick sustainers:** One for each container.
- **Double boiler**
- **Thermometer**
- **Ladle and/or vessel for pouring:** Preferably with a handle.
- **Small sticks:** A dowel, chopsticks, or even a slim garden stake will work for suspending the wick over the container.
- **Weights:** You need to weigh down the wick in the container if you're using a non-cored variety; small washers or nuts will work fine.
- **Utensil for poking holes in the wax:** This can be a skewer, chopstick, pencil, or small stick.

## STEPS TO MAKING A CONTAINER CANDLE

Assemble all your tools and materials in the order in which you'll be using them before you begin your candle making operation. You don't want to have the wax melted and then start looking for a container or another needed tool.

*Throughout this process, keep a close eye on your thermometer. Make sure the wax is not overheating while you prepare the wick and container for pouring.*

1. Measure the wax. To ascertain how much wax is needed to fill your container (or containers, if you're making multiples), fill the container with water and pour the water into a measuring cup to determine the container's volume, then dry the container thoroughly.

2. Begin melting wax in your double boiler.

3. After the wax has reached the proper melting point (usually 150°F–160°F), prime your wick as directed earlier in this chapter.

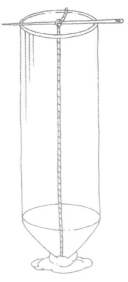

**Figure 5-3:**
*The dowel and the wick*

4. Attach a wick sustainer to the primed wick. Put the wick sustainer on one end; this will be the bottom. If you're using an un-cored wick, you will need to tie your small weight to the wick to ensure it stays anchored while pouring the wax.

5. Lay the dowel or chopstick across the top of your container. Tie the top end of the wick to it so the wick hangs steadily in the container.

6. Warm the container before pouring wax into it. You can do this one of several ways: place it in a warming oven (150°F) for a few minutes; put it in the sink and run hot water into it; or set a pan of water on the stove over low heat and put the container (or containers) in the water to warm it before use. Make sure the container is dried thoroughly before use.

*If you're using glass containers, warm them slowly (the hot water method is safest). If metal, don't let them get so hot they burn your fingers. Always use a hot pad to handle a heated container.*

7. If you're adding stearin to pure paraffin, add it to the wax now and stir well.

8. Begin pouring slowly to one side of the dowel holding the wick. Make sure you keep the wick centered in the container, using the bottom tab or weight to do so.

You may need to hold it in place for a few moments to allow it to set. This "tack pour," of about ½" of wax in the bottom of the container, is an important step, as a wick that is off-center will cause the candle to burn lopsidedly. Allow the ½" of wax at the bottom to cool enough to stabilize the centered wick.

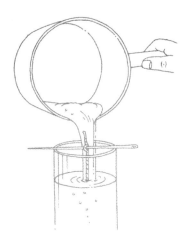

**Figure 5-4:**
*Pouring the wax*

9. Once the tack pour has cooled, continue pouring the wax until it's about ½" from the top.

10. Wait a few minutes for the wax to begin to congeal. Then, with your skewer, poke a few holes into the cooling wax. Pour a bit more wax into these holes. This second pour (the "repour" or "cap pour") fills in spaces caused by air bubbles that formed during the first pour.

11. Repeat the repouring process until the wax cools.

12. Wax shrinks as it cools and the candle will develop a depression in the center. Pour more melted wax into this

depression when the candle is firm to the touch in order to make a flat surface.

13. When the candle has cooled completely (this takes anywhere from 8–24 hours, depending on the candle's diameter), trim the wick to ⅓" above the candle's surface.

# CHAPTER 6

# CROSS-STITCH AND SEWING

Working with needle and thread is a relaxing and beneficial task. Not only can you create something beautiful and practical but you can have fun doing it! This chapter will take you through the basics of cross-stitch and how to create a cross-stitch project of your own. You'll also learn how to sew your own curtains. The curtain making projects in this chapter are not for novice sewers who have never ventured past sewing on a button, but if you have basic sewing knowledge, you should be more than capable of handling them.

## Cross-Stitching

To learn about the art of cross-stitching, try this happy mushroom cross-stitch pattern. This sweet mushroom design is an easy beginner project with large areas of color for satisfying stitching.

**For this project you will need:**

- 11-count Aida cloth (10" × 10")
- Embroidery scissors
- 1 skein, 6-strand embroidery floss, DMC brand #321 Red
- 1 skein, 6-strand embroidery floss, DMC brand #704 Chartreuse–Bright
- 1 skein, 6-strand embroidery floss, DMC brand #911 Emerald Green–Medium
- 1 skein, 6-strand embroidery floss, DMC brand #3864 Mocha Beige–Light
- 1 skein, 6-strand embroidery floss, DMC brand #3862 Mocha Beige–Dark
- 1 skein, 6-strand embroidery floss, DMC brand #B5200 Snow White
- 1 size 24 tapestry needle
- 1 straight pin to mark center of fabric
- 1 pencil or highlighter

Here is a quick explanation of some of the materials used.

## FABRIC

This project uses 11-count Aida cloth. Aida fabric is a woven cloth that has squares with stitching holes in each corner. The count refers to the number of stitches in an inch. An 11-count weave has 11 cross stitches in every inch. As you progress in expertise, try a higher count, such as 12- or 14-count Aida cloth.

### EMBROIDERY SCISSORS

Embroidery scissors are smaller than regular scissors with long thin blades and sharp tips that fit into small places. Use them exclusively for fabric, floss, and thread so the blades stay sharp for quick, clean snips. Using the scissors on paper will dull them.

### EMBROIDERY FLOSS

This project uses DMC brand embroidery floss that's made up of six twisted strands in an 8.7-yard skein. This project uses three strands to make a thread on a needle. DMC is available in a large variety of colors and is packaged in skeins that can be re-wrapped onto embroidery thread bobbins for storage and organization.

### NEEDLES

Use a size 24 tapestry needle. The needle number refers to the needle's dimension, length, and the size of its eye. A tapestry needle has a blunt end and is easy to thread. The French brand Bohin is recommended due to the ease with which it weaves through cloth.

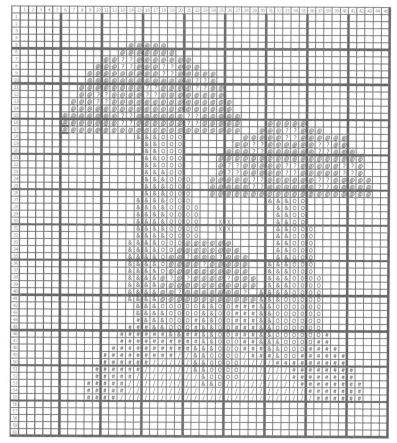

**Figure 6-1:** *Happy mushrooms cross-stitch pattern*

## HOOP (OPTIONAL)

Some stitchers prefer to stitch in a wooden or plastic hoop or a Q-Snap (PVC) frame, but for this project, the Aida fabric is stiff enough to simply hold in hand.

## Preparing the Fabric and Finding the Center

Before you begin this project, cut a 10" × 10" square of Aida fabric. The measurement includes a 2"–3" border around the finished project. After the fabric is cut to size, find the center by first folding it in half in one direction, pinching the crease, then opening the fabric and folding it in half in the other direction. Insert a straight pin where the folds intersect to mark the center.

## How to Read the Pattern

In order to read the pattern, there are a few things you need to know.

### DESIGN COUNT

The numbers for the design count refer to how many stitches fill the length and height of the stitch pattern. The count of the fabric determines the finished size of the cross-stitch design. The project here is 51 stitches high by 38 stitches wide using an Aida cloth with 11 stitches per inch, therefore $51 \div 11 = 4.64"$ and $38 \div 11 = 3.45"$.

### COLOR KEY

The pattern has a color key that shows the colors and amounts of floss needed. In addition, each color has a corresponding symbol so the pattern can be printed in black and white. Here's the color key for this pattern:

| Skeins Needed | DMC Number | Color Name | Symbol |
|:---:|:---:|:---:|:---:|
| 1 | 321 | Red | @ |
| 1 | 704 | Chartreuse—Bright | # |
| 1 | 911 | Emerald Green—Medium | / |
| 1 | 3864 | Mocha Beige—Light | O |
| 1 | 3862 | Mocha Beige—Dark | & |
| 1 | B5200 | Snow White | ʔ |

## THE GRID

The pattern has a grid separated into five- and ten-square sections. Use a highlighter or pencil to keep track of finished squares in the pattern.

## Separating Strands

Cross-stitching is done with a different number of strands, depending on the design. The recommended brand of embroidery floss for this project (DMC) has six strands, which will need to be separated into two groups, each with three strands. To separate the strands:

1. Measure and cut a length of floss that stretches from fingertip to elbow, about 12"–18". A longer thread can get rough from running through the fabric and will tangle and knot; a shorter thread will require frequent needle reloading.
2. With your finger, tap the ends of the floss to "flower the thread" (spread the ends out like a flower) to gently separate half of the strands (three).
3. Place a finger between the two sections and slowly run it down between the two separate strand groups. Thread one (three-strand) group through the needle.

**Tips:** After the floss is separated into a group of three strands, thread the second strand group onto a second needle. It makes for a faster setup and the thread is less likely to be misplaced.

## Stitches and Stitch Direction

A cross-stitch is an X-shaped embroidery stitch. As a beginner, it's easiest to make stitches one of two ways: the English method or the Danish method.

*Two tips to keep in mind when stitching: Dangle thread and needle to get rid of the twists that come from stitching and aim for consistent tension with stitches (they should lie flat against the fabric).*

## ENGLISH METHOD

With the English method, complete each individual whole cross-stitch. Make each X stitch before moving to the next stitch and stay consistent in the way the stitch is layered. Here's how:

1. To start, bring the needle out in the lower left corner (hole 1).
2. Move the needle up and across to the opposite right side corner, come down and in (hole 2).

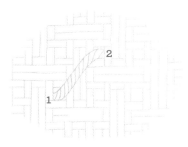

**Figure 6-2:** *English method step 2*

3. Bring the needle back out through the bottom right corner (hole 3).

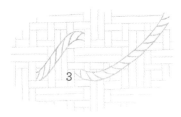

**Figure 6-3:** *English method step 3*

4. Move the needle over and into the last hole (4) in the top left corner.

Figure 6-4: *English method step 4*

Figure 6-5: *Finished English method stitch*

## DANISH METHOD

Make a half stitch in one direction (holes 1 to 2) for a length of squares, then return back (holes 3 to 4) in the other direction, finishing the X shape.

**Figure 6-6:** *Danish method step 1*

**Figure 6-7:** *Danish method step 2*

The Danish method is easy for large areas both horizontal and vertical, but the most important thing is to be consistent in stitch overlap order no matter which method is used. It doesn't matter how the stitch is made as long as the order is consistent.

## Starting and Ending

Cross-stitch is usually done working in rows from left to right. Find the center of the fabric and count to where you want to begin, then anchor using a pin stitch. The pin stitch is a very useful way to anchor the thread because it hides under a cross-stitch.

### To make a pin stitch:
1. From the back side, insert the needle out into the middle of the square you'll be starting in.
2. Pull the thread up and, staying within the center of the square, move the needle to the back of the fabric.
3. Move to the corner of the square and start the first stitch in the design, thus covering that square with a normal X stitch.

To end, gently weave the needle through several stitches on the back side and trim.

## Making Your Own Curtains

Making your own curtains is not only more economical than buying ready-made ones but also allows you the satisfaction of crafting something beautiful with your own hands. In addition, you'll be able to choose the colors and textures that best suit your home and aesthetic. Check catalogs and magazines for ideas. Different fabric combinations, lengths, trims, and shapes might inspire you to greater creativity. But, before you rush to the fabric store to buy your fabric, you need to make a few decisions.

- Will the room benefit from having the curtains extend beyond the window or should the outside edge of the woodwork be visible around the curtain?
- Do you want the curtains to hover just above the sill, hang to the bottom of the lower edge of the woodwork or apron, or hang clear to the floor? Perhaps they belong somewhere in between?
- Do you want sheer curtains to diffuse the light or heavier ones to block it? Or are you more interested in a window treatment for its decorative value?
- Should they be a solid color to bring out a single color in the room or a print to tie several colors or neutral tones together?

Your answers to these questions will help you determine the type and location of your hardware and the type of fabric and style of curtain you choose.

We will begin with simple shirred curtains, the most basic type of curtains. The top of the curtain is hemmed with a casing through which the curtain rod is inserted, gathering the curtain along its length. Shirred curtains will not slide open and closed easily, though they are often tied at the sides, framing the window with a graceful draped effect. They are also not appropriate for very heavy fabrics because of the difficulty of gathering them on a rod. Most other curtains use some of the same construction techniques as the shirred.

## Choosing Fabrics and Estimating Yardage

There are a few general things to consider as you shop for fabric. To make this easier, let's begin with some fabric and fabric store terms.

- Fabric is generally sold by the yard or fraction of a yard and is sometimes referred to as yard goods. It is usually displayed at the store in large rolls called bolts.
- The tightly woven edges of the fabric are called selvages. The threads that run parallel to them are called lengthwise or warp threads.
- The cut edge is called the raw edge and the threads running along that direction are called crosswise or weft threads.
- The bias is an imaginary line running diagonally across these two threads at a 45-degree angle. This line has the most stretch.

When you go to a fabric store, you'll see a wide variety of fabrics to choose from. Besides fabrics that are too heavy to shirr, there are a few other things to avoid. Pure cotton fabrics are sensitive to the sun and fade rather quickly. If your curtains will catch any direct sunlight, cotton polyester blends will last longer. They have a crisper look as well. If you like the rustic look of cotton, choose linen or undyed muslin.

Also avoid prints that have any kind of noticeable horizontal design unless it's woven in. If a printed design is off grain, it will make your entire window treatment look crooked, and if you try to cut your curtain with the print rather than the grain, your curtains will never hang in straight folds.

### ESTIMATING YARDAGE

Another consideration should be the weight of the fabric. The more sheer the fabric, the fuller the curtains should be. Usually the width of the curtain or curtain pair is twice the width of the curtain rod. Heavier curtains might only be one and a half times the width and sheer curtains can be three times as wide.

Decide whether you want one straight curtain that hangs over the window at all times (or is pulled to one side for an asymmetrical look) or if you want two panels that meet in the center and are tied back or dropped into place as desired. Curtains on doors or casement windows are often shirred at the bottom as well as the top. Determine the placement of the lower rod and use it when figuring your measurements. Next, decide on the length of the curtains. To this length, add 4" for a top hem and casing or 7" if you want a 1½" heading. (A heading is a small ridge of ruffled curtain above the casing.) Add more if you have a wide, flat curtain rod. Also add 6" for a bottom hem. You can make narrower hems but the extra fabric adds crispness to the top and weight to the bottom. If you're using a bottom rod, add the length for its casing instead of the lower hem.

If piecing is necessary, the seams should be on the vertical to hide among the folds. The width of your curtains in relation to the width of your fabric will tell you how many of the figured lengths of fabric you'll need. Since selvages sometimes shrink, you will be trimming them away, reducing the fabric's width by at least ½". Another ½" of width will be lost if you are piecing two and 1" will be lost from the width of a middle length if you are piecing three. There will be 2" used on each side of each curtain for hems, further reducing the width of your fabric lengths. If you need just under one and a half times the width of the fabric to make each of two curtains, you will need three times the total length of your finished curtains, plus 10" for the hems. In other words, plan to use a length for each curtain and a third length to split between the two. Add 1" or so per yard for possible shrinkage and you have an approximation of the yardage you'll need.

## Cutting Out Your Curtains

If your curtain fabric is washable, preshrink it. Next, you'll need to straighten your fabric. Straightening fabric simply means putting the lengthwise and crosswise threads into as perpendicular a position as possible. Before you can check to see if your fabric needs to be straightened, you must trim one raw edge of your fabric along a thread line.

If your fabric has woven stripes, checks, or plaids, you can simply follow one of the stripes. For other fabrics, clip through the selvage near the edge and pull a thread until it breaks. Cut along the line you've created. Pull a thread again, trim, and so on across to the other selvage. One edge of your fabric is now cut along the crosswise threads. Fold this line in half to determine if the selvages are perpendicular. If they hang together when you hold up the folded end, your fabric is straight with the grain.

If they do not hang together, pull on the appropriate diagonal all along the length of your fabric. Remember, the true bias isn't going to be corner to corner unless your fabric is exactly as long as it is wide. To determine which direction to pull, notice which edge of your fabric is hanging closer to the center fold. That is the edge that needs to be pulled outward from the opposite corner above.

Knits don't have weft and warp threads; instead, they have lengthwise and crosswise stitches. Pulling a thread is not going to be possible. Cut the end following a row of stitches as closely as possible. It may be easier to follow a row from the back of the fabric. Test the same way you would woven fabric. Pull very gently on the bias to straighten.

A great many yards of fabric will be difficult to straighten all at once, so pull threads to cut your fabric into lengths and straighten them individually. If you have a pattern to match, simply start each length at exactly the same place in the pattern, cut it to the correct length (the finished curtain plus your hem and heading allowances), then cut away the fabric to the next pattern repeat.

With the lengths cut out and straightened, cut away all selvage edges. Split any lengths that are wider than necessary. You can usually pull lengthwise threads to make a straight cut.

*If you want curtains that open and close easily but don't want the trouble of pleats and hooks, make your curtains as if to shirr them, only without a heading. Use curtain rings with tiny clamps to hang your curtains. They are available from home decorating catalogs and from some well-stocked department stores.*

## Sewing Your Curtains

If your fabric is the right width for your curtains, you're ready to hem them. If not, begin by piecing the lengths together.

*For pressing your fabrics, an iron (preferably with steam) and an ironing board are absolute necessities. Your ironing board doesn't have to be a full-sized one; a small version that sits on a table will do fine. A sleeve board that looks a little like a miniature ironing board is used for narrow items such as cuffs and sleeves. A point presser is a wooden stand that looks like an anvil. It's used to press points into collars and other turned points.*

## PIECING YOUR CURTAINS

The best way to seam your lengths together is with a French seam. Begin by deciding where these seams should be. Typically, the narrower length should be toward the outside of the window to be less noticeable. Take care to keep all printed designs or textures in the right direction.

To make a French seam, pin your two lengths of fabric together with the wrong sides together. Sew a narrow ¼" seam along the edge. Press the seam open, then turn the fabric right sides together and press the seam again. If the fabric wants to slide, pin the seam. Sew a second seam ⅜" from the first seam to hide the raw edge within the seam. Press the seam flat against the curtain.

## HEMMING THE SIDES

Press the sides of each panel under 2". A sewing gauge is very helpful here. Fold the raw edge under to the fold line. If you're after a country or rustic look, you can straight-stitch the side hems close to the fold. For a more formal curtain, either use the hemstitch on your machine or do the hems by hand.

## MAKING THE CASINGS AND HEADINGS

If you didn't include extra fabric for a heading, press the top of the curtain panels under 4", then press the raw edge under in line with the crease. Pin the hem carefully so the corners of the top casing's hem don't extend beyond the side hems. Hemstitch with your machine or by hand.

If you added extra fabric for a heading, press the raw edge under 5½", then press the raw edge under 2". Sew close to the hem edge with a straight or hemstitch. Sew another row of stitches 1½" from the top edge. This will define the heading and the casing for the rod will be below it. Either set up a temporary guide on your machine for sewing 1½" from the edge or mark the stitching line with pins or chalk.

*If you're pressing a double fold for a hem, you can press the edge under and fold it over again but it won't be as accurate as folding the full amount under first. It's hard to see exactly what you're doing with the second fold.*

## HEMMING THE BOTTOM

Before you hem the bottom of your curtains, compare the panels. Put them wrong sides together to compare the center and outside lengths. Trim one if necessary. Compare again after the hem is pressed under and before you stitch it. If you're anchoring your curtain with a rod on the bottom, make the bottom casing the same way you did the top. If you allowed 6" for the bottom hem, press the raw edge under that amount, then press the raw edge to the fold line. This hem can be stitched the same way the upper casing was. Or, to be sure the hem allowance doesn't stick out beyond the sides, you can fold the corners under. To do this, fold only as far as the side hemstitching, as shown in Figure 6-8. Be sure the lower corner is still sharp. Blindstitch along the diagonal crease to keep it from coming out.

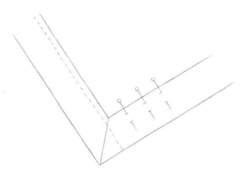

**Figure 6-8:** *Hemmed corner: Turn under the end but keep the corner sharp*

In some situations, such as when an air vent is directly under your curtains, you might want to add more weight to the lower hem. There are chain weights made for this purpose, or you can use a length of ball chain like those used for light pulls. Run them through the hem and stitch them at each end. You can also use metal washers in the corners but plan to remove them when you wash the curtains or they might rust and stain the fabric. Be careful also that you don't use weights so heavy they stretch your curtains or tear the hem.

## Making Ruffles

Ruffles on curtains may seem too frilly in certain applications, but in bathrooms, breakfast areas, or kitchens, they can add a cheerful touch. You might find a ready-made eyelet or cotton ruffle that works perfectly with your curtain plans, but generally you'll need to make your own from the curtain fabric or a coordinating one.

### MEASURING THE RUFFLES

Ruffles often run along the inside edges and across the bottoms of a pair of curtains. Sometimes the ruffles are only on the bottoms. Another row of ruffles can be sewn just below the casing but more often a valance is made to mimic the fullness of the ruffle and shirred onto the outer portion of a double rod.

When you decide how to use your ruffles, take their width into account when measuring for your curtains. A bottom ruffle will take the place of a hem as well as add length to the curtains. The ruffle itself can be from 3"–8" wide and, depending on the weight of the fabric, anywhere from double to triple the length of the curtain it's gathered against. Consider, too, if you want your ruffle to have a heading. This would be 1" of ruffle fabric above the gathering stitches, making a small decorative head to the ruffle.

If you will be making your own ruffle instead of buying it ready-made, consider the weight of your ruffle fabric. Lighter-weight fabric is usually cut twice the width of the needed ruffle, plus 1". Include the heading, if any, in this measurement. Stiffer, heavier fabrics are usually hemmed on both sides and only need to be cut 1" wider than your ruffle and heading will be.

Don't try to guess how much ruffle fabric you'll need. Figure out how many strips of fabric with a width of 42" you'll need and multiply that by the width of fabric needed for the ruffle. Remember to account for piecing seams and trimming off the selvages. If, at the store, you discover your fabric's width is much different than 42", do some refiguring.

## CUTTING AND HEMMING RUFFLES

Cut your ruffle fabric into the strips you calculated. If you're folding your ruffles double, you can stitch the strips together with ½" straight seams and press the allowances open. Fold the entire ruffle, right sides together, and stitch ½" from the raw edge. Turn the tube right side out. A large safety pin fastened to the seam allowance can help with the turning if your ruffle is narrow. Iron the ruffle flat with the seam running along the center of one side. Turn the raw edges of the ends ½" inside the tube, press, and stitch the ends.

If you're hemming your ruffle, piece the strips together with French seams as described for piecing the curtain panels. Press these seams to one side. Hem the bottom edge of the ruffle lengths using ½" of fabric or with a hemming foot attachment for your sewing machine. (If your machine came with this type of presser foot, here's your chance to try it!) If you've allowed for a heading, hem both long sides of your ruffle.

*You can make tie-backs for your curtains using the same stitch-and-turn method described for making ruffles. Cut your fabric twice the width of your desired ties plus 1". Cut one long strip that equals the length you want each of your ties to be plus ½", times the number of ties. Stitch and turn, then cut the ties apart.*

### GATHERING THE RUFFLE

Make two rows of long machine stitches ¼" apart where your ruffle needs to gather. If your ruffle does not have a heading, these rows of stitches will be ¼" and ½" from the edge. If you're making a ruffle with a heading, these rows will be just under and just over 1" from the edge.

### ATTACHING A RUFFLE WITH A HEADING

Hem the side or sides of your curtain that will not have a ruffle as described earlier. Press the casing hem under but do not stitch it. The edges of the curtain that will be decorated with a ruffle need to be turned and hemmed. This can be done toward the front if you want because the ruffle will cover it, thus giving the back of the curtain a more finished look.

Pin the ruffle to the curtain, wrong side of ruffle to right side of curtain, with the rows of gathering stitches running along or just above the hem. Distribute the extra ruffle fabric as evenly as possible over the curtain edge. If the ruffle is going around a corner, allow extra fullness so the ruffle doesn't turn under. Extend the ruffle only to the point where the curtain will fold for the top casing.

Use a pin to pull the ruffling stitches and gather the fabric until it lies flat between the pins. Topstitch along both rows of gathering stitches. If you're running a row of ruffles along the top of your curtain, either above or below the casing, stitch the casing down as described earlier. Gather the ruffle onto the width of the curtain and attach the same as described previously.

*Pleated drapes and lined curtains are not projects that should be tackled by beginners. The problems aren't so much the techniques as the unique sewing problems caused by heavy drapery fabric, heat-resistant lining, and crinoline or other stiffening products needed for the pleats.*

## ATTACHING A RUFFLE WITHOUT A HEADING

If your ruffle is double-folded, the gathering edge is finished and your ruffle can be attached just like the ruffle with the heading except you'll be stitching close to the edge. However, if your gathering stitches are along the raw edge of a single-thickness ruffle, you'll need to attach the ruffle in such a way as to cover the raw edge. This same method can be followed for a folded ruffle if you want a more finished look.

For ruffles accenting the bottom or side edges of the curtains, begin by pressing the raw edge of the curtain ¾" from back to front, then press the raw edge under ¼". Do not stitch. Lay your ruffle on the curtain, right sides together, with the bottom edge of the ruffle pointed toward the center of the curtain. Line up the raw edge of the ruffle with the inside fold on the curtain edge. Gather and stitch as described for the headed ruffle, being sure to allow extra fullness if you're gathering around a corner.

Turn the pressed edges of the curtain up over the gathers and stitch close to the edge. There's no perfect way to do this around the corner, so just try to be sure all raw edges are tucked under. The ruffle should fall into place. Iron the curtain away from the ruffle. You may want to topstitch the finished ruffle end to the curtain.

If you're attaching a row of ruffles to the surface of your curtain, cut a length of extra-wide double-fold bias tape ½" longer than the width of the curtain. Open out the first fold and stitch the ends under ¼". Pin your ruffle to the tape, lining up the raw edge with the center fold on the bias tape. Gather and stitch, then turn the bias tape over the gathers and stitch. Sew this tape-edged ruffle along the casing after it's been hemmed in place.

*Why not finish the top edge before you gather it? The three layers of fabric at the edge of the ruffle created by turning it under will not gather the same as the single layer of fabric below it where the other row of gathering stitches will be. In fact, it won't gather well at all.*

## Making Valances and Flounces

Valances are generally a separate curtain shirred onto the outer portion of a double curtain rod. The straight-bottom ones are made just like the curtains, but there are other possibilities. Some elaborately draped window valances are actually made with no sewing except on the hems. The trick is to give yourself the right fullness and length to drape them the way you want. Also, be willing to do a little hand sewing from the top of a stepladder to keep them that way.

### SWAG- OR SCALLOPED-SHAPED VALANCES

Swag-shaped valances extend far down the window on the outside edges and angle dramatically upward to a narrow valance at the center. These are made by cutting the fabric into the desired shape and adding a narrow hem or finishing the edge. Make your pattern on heavy tissue or on the brown paper you find sold in rolls (usually in the aisle with packing materials).

Pin your pattern to the fabric and cut both sides at once. Be sure your fabric is lying with either right sides or wrong sides together so you get a right side and a left side for your curtains. If you're using fabric that's exactly the same on the front and back, you may be able to cut your curtain the desired length and top width, then cut it in half diagonally to get both sides. If you're doing two identical windows and your fabric has no one-way effect, cut one from lower right to upper left and the other from lower left to upper right.

The more complicated scalloped, curved, or pointed valances are done with lining. Design your shape to fit your window and cut out the shape from your fabric. Cut out a second identical shape from a neutral fabric that will not show through your curtain fabric. Put the lining right side down on the right side of your curtain and stitch around the lower curves and the sides.

**Figure 6-9:** *Points: Stitch across a point rather than into it—one stitch across the corner on lightweight fabric, two or more on heavier fabrics*

To make sharp points, stitch across the corner (see Figure 6-9). Thin fabrics will only require one stitch across the point while thicker fabrics will require two or even three. Trim away the seam allowance close to the stitches so there's less bulk inside the point.

Grade the seam allowances by cutting the lining's allowance to one half the allowance of the curtain. Clip inward curves almost to the stitching line and outward curves with a V. Turn the curtain right side out and press the lower edges and sides. Rolling the edge between your thumb and finger can sometimes help you turn the seam completely. Treat the two layers as one when you make the top casing.

*Valances that have a draped or pulled look are made by curving the top edge. It's difficult to guess exactly how such a valance will hang. It can also be a bit tricky to sew the casing on a curve but the gathers when it's shirred on a rod will hide the puckers.*

## MOCK VALANCES AND FLOUNCES

Sometimes a valance is actually part of the lower curtains but is made to appear as if it's separate. This is generally done by making the casing part of the valance, then gathering the valance onto the top of the curtain just below the casing. If your window is large enough for an even fuller look, consider overlapping the curtains under the valance. Both sides can be pulled back with ties once the curtains are hung. Flounces are made similarly to the mock valances, except the lower edge is caught up to the curtain close to the casing, leaving a loop of fabric to puff out. This seam is actually sewn to the curtains proper before the top of the curtains are attached to the valance.

## Tab Curtains

Tab curtains are hung on decorative rods by loops or tabs made from fabric or ribbons attached to the top of the curtain. They're usually not as full as shirred curtains so they require less fabric. Different tabs will give your curtains different looks. How many tabs you use and their widths will determine how far you'll be able to slide the curtains open.

To make your own tabs, cut a strip of fabric to the desired width times two, plus 1" for the seam. The length will depend on the size of your curtain rod and how much drop you want between the rod and the top of your curtain. Take the desired distance from the top of the rod to the curtains times two, plus 1" and the approximate diameter of the rod. This will give you the length you need for each tab. Take this measurement times the number of tabs for the length of fabric you need to cut.

The tab strip is sewn and turned the same way as the doubled-over ruffle. Press the strip flat with the seam down the center of one side and cut it to the proper lengths. Fold the tabs in half and space them on the right side of your curtains after the side seams have been hemmed. Line up the raw edges of the tabs with the raw edge of the curtain top and the loop ends toward the center of the curtain. Stitch them in place ¼" from the edge. Cut a facing piece the width of your curtains plus 1" for side hems and approximately 4" long. Put narrow hems on the sides of your facing using ½" on each side.

Stitch the facing to the top of the curtain right sides together about ½" from the raw edge. The tabs will be between the two layers. Trim the seam allowance of the facing to about ¼". Turn the facing to the wrong side and press. Fold the bottom edge of the facing under and hemstitch it to the curtain.

## Scalloped-Topped Curtains

Some curtains, usually café curtains with tabs or peaks clipped to rings, will have scallops between the tabs or rings. To make scallops, cut the curtains allowing an extra 6" or so at the top to fold back for lining. The amount you need to allow will depend on the depth of your scallops. Also, if you plan to fold back the top for tabs, remember to allow the total length of the tab in both the curtains and the lining.

After the side hems are sewn, turn the top down toward the front by the amount you allowed for your lining. Pin it both at the bottom edge and across the fold to hold it securely. Make a pattern for the scallops. These can be a half circle if you're attaching your curtains to rings or much deeper for tabs. Space them evenly across the top of the curtain, about 1" apart. Mark the scallops with a pencil or chalk.

Being sure the fabric stays flat on the fold, stitch along the marked scallops. Cut away the half circles to within ¼" of the stitching and clip the curves. Turn the lining to the back and gently push out the peaks or tabs. Press. Turn the tabs under the appropriate length and hand stitch to the lining.

# CHAPTER 7

# QUILTING AND EMBROIDERY

C urling up with a cozy quilt is one of the joys of life and making one for yourself is a creative endeavor to be proud of. This chapter will take you through the steps of making your own quilt, from basic quilting terms and equipment to choosing your fabric and using the correct stitches. You'll also learn about following patterns before trying your hand at two homemade projects. If you're intrigued about the art of quilting, this chapter will put you on the right path.

## Quilting Basics

Although there are exceptions, the basic quilt consists of three layers. The first is the backing, or bottom, layer, which is generally made of a plain fabric and is sometimes called a lining. The term *backing* is less confusing because no other part of a quilt or quilted project is likely to be referred to as such, while *lining* might refer to other things.

The middle layer is the batting. This gives the quilt its insulating properties. The thickness of the batting combined with the style of stitching determines how heavy or puffy the quilt will be. This middle layer is sometimes called the filling or padding but these terms bring to mind more old-fashioned products than the commercial quilt batting used in modern quilts.

The third and final layer is the cover. This is the decorated layer often called a quilt top or, more rarely, the face. Since *top* might refer to the headboard end of the finished quilt and *face* can be confused with *facing*, the term *cover* is somewhat preferable and is what will be used in this chapter.

## TYPES OF QUILTS

There are two primary types of quilts: pieced and appliquéd. Pieced refers to a quilt cover made up of many (sometimes hundreds of) small pieces of cloth stitched together. These pieces might go together to create one large pattern such as a star on the cover. More often, the pieces are arranged in repeating geometric patterns. Sometimes these patterns are alternately turned to one side or another, or dark and light colors are used to create diamond or stripe effects.

Appliquéd quilts are made of cutout shapes stitched onto a contrasting background. If the design consists of one large picture, it is said to have an allover pattern. Often the appliquéd picture is repeated, much like the pieced pattern, and sewn onto blocks, which are then sewn together.

A comforter (or comfortable, as it was called some hundred years ago) is a tied quilt, which means, instead of rows of stitching joining the layers together, threads are caught through the layers at even intervals and tied in knots. It's a quilt that isn't quilted. A plain quilt, on the other hand, is exceedingly quilted. The cover is made from one solid-colored piece, often white, and this is where it gets its name. It's then quilted all over in the most intricate of patterns, typically very detailed garlands of flowers, feathered wreaths, or figures of animals, people, houses, or ships.

## CONSTRUCTION OF A QUILT

"Pattern" refers to the guide you will follow to make your quilt but also the design itself. The pattern (guide) will show you how to cut the pieces that will make up a particular pattern (design). Sometimes a template (a cardboard or plastic cutout) is used to cut the pieces. Sewing these pieces together along a seam line is called piecing. Sewing one piece on top of another is called appliquéing.

If the pattern repeats across the cover of the quilt, each of these repetitions is called a block. Sometimes blocks are sewn together directly while sometimes they're separated by a strip of fabric called a panel. When the blocks and panels are sewn together, it is referred to as setting the quilt. When the layers of the quilt are put together, it is called assembling the quilt.

Often there are strips of cloth sewn around the outside edges of the set blocks. These are called borders. The size of borders can be easily changed, which is handy if the pattern you're using isn't going to make your quilt quite the size you want. Borders can be plain, designed to frame a fancy quilt, or very intricately pieced, appliquéd, or stitched. Sometimes they're intended to be the part of the quilt that hangs over the edge of the bed and therefore are present only on the sides and bottom of the quilt. The top (the headboard end) is finished with the top row of blocks or with a narrow border. The process of finishing the raw edges around the quilt is called binding. The material used for this purpose is called binding as well.

Stitching that's used to hold pieces or layers together temporarily until more thorough stitching can be completed is called basting. The tiny decorative stitching that holds the layers together and gives the quilt its distinctive beauty is the quilting stitch.

## Quilting Tools and Supplies

Quilting shops and catalogs offer many marvelous gadgets for the quilter that can simplify part of the process or make cutting or sewing more accurate, yet you can begin quilting with very little expense. After all, the original quilters did without these modern "necessities." Consider getting more advanced equipment as your hobby expands and start only with these essentials.

### PINS AND NEEDLES

Needles and pins are the most basic of quilting tools and everyone, even a non-sewer, will most likely have a few somewhere in their home. Needles come in numbered sizes. The larger the number, the smaller the diameter of the needle. To quilt, you will need two distinct kinds of needles, each for a separate type of sewing: sharps and betweens.

- **Sharps:** Sharps are the most common type of needle. They are called sharps because they begin tapering right below the eye, becoming narrower all the way to their sharp point. You'll use sharps for basting, piecing, and any other hand sewing you do besides the quilting itself. Sizes 7 and 8 are your best choices for this work.

- **Betweens:** The needles you should use for quilting are called betweens. The most common theory as to how they got their name is that they are somewhere between the sharp and darning needle in characteristics. They don't taper like the sharps but come to a sudden point very close to the end. Size 7 or 8 is recommended. The finer the needle, the smaller the holes left in the fabric and the more easily it will glide through the layers. Some experienced quilters even prefer size 9 needles.

- **Pins:** Extra-fine pins are best for quilting because they leave smaller holes in your fabric. Pins with ball heads, as opposed to standard flathead pins, are desirable because they're less likely to catch threads as you sew. The colored glass–headed pins are better still because they're easy to find in your work (unless, of course, you accidentally match a pin to a piece of fabric).

## THREAD

The thread is what holds your quilt together. If a thread breaks in your finished quilt, you'll have a hole that is difficult to mend effectively. Part of a seam's strength comes from the stitch you use but the rest comes from the thread itself. This is why it's important to consider the type of thread you'll use for your quilts. Here are some options:

- **All-purpose thread:** Basic all-purpose thread is what you'll use for piecing, appliqué, and all other stitching apart from the quilting itself. As a general rule, try to use a color of thread that matches the fabric you're sewing. If an exact match isn't possible, a shade lighter is less noticeable than a shade darker. When piecing—that is, stitching together two pieces of fabric—the thread will be hidden within the seam and will not show from the outside unless it's vastly different from the fabric. If you're working with many different colors of fabric, there's no need to switch threads with each pair of pieces. A light shade similar to the lightest fabric or an appropriate hue of gray or tan should blend with all of them. The color of your thread becomes especially important with appliqué because the thread will be visible. Try to match the fabric exactly and switch colors with each piece unless you want the stitching to accent the pieces.
- **Basting thread:** Basting should be done with a contrasting color for ease in finding the threads that need to be removed. Avoid very dark colors as they may leave behind

tiny specks of cotton coating that are difficult to brush away.

- **Quilting thread:** You will need a stronger thread made especially for quilting. Besides being more durable, this stiffer thread is less prone to tangling. Quilting thread is sold in most sewing departments and comes in many colors, as well as the standard white. Whether your quilting stitches blend or contrast with the fabric is a matter of choice.

You will also find special thread made for machine quilting. If you decide you'll be doing a great deal of machine quilting, you might want to give it a try. Otherwise, what little machine quilting you'll be doing can be done with all-purpose thread.

## SEWING SCISSORS

While everyone has scissors in their homes, getting the appropriate scissors for quilting might be worth the investment. Trying to cut fabric with dull scissors will not only frustrate you but also make your pieces fray and interfere with the accuracy of your cutting. It could easily affect the appearance of the finished quilt. Here are some options:

- **Fabric shears:** Any good-quality shears will do fine. Buy a new pair, if possible, and mark them in some way as your fabric shears. Never use them for anything else.
- **Thread scissors:** A handy addition to your sewing basket (but not a necessity) is a pair of small scissors for clipping

threads. You'll find them so much easier to handle than general-use scissors for the quick snip at either the sewing machine or the quilt frame.

- **Rotary cutter:** One gadget that can be worth the investment is the rotary cutter. A rotary cutter has a circular blade that works much like a pizza cutter. It's always used with a cutting mat and often with a clear ruler.

## RULERS

You will need, at the very least, a 6" ruler with ¹⁄₁₆" markings and something longer for measuring the larger pieces. A yardstick works well for this purpose. There are acrylic rulers that are extremely handy for cutting quilting pieces and they come in a variety of sizes. A 6" × 6" square ruler and another that's 18" long are recommended if you're able to invest in them.

## THIMBLES

Thimbles are intended to protect the finger that pushes the thread through the fabric from becoming sore or even punctured by the eye end of the needle. Thimbles are generally worn on the middle finger.

Sometimes a second thimble is worn on the hand under the quilt. This hand helps push the needle back up through the quilt and might need the protection of a thimble as well. The standard metal thimble is the most readily available and probably the best choice for a beginner. Once you've settled on the type of thimble to start with, check for a correct fit. It shouldn't squeeze the fingertip but it also shouldn't fall off easily.

 *If your fingernails are keeping your thimble from fitting comfortably, don't cut them off yet. There are special thimbles designed to accommodate long fingernails. Look for them in quilt shops and catalogs.*

## PATTERN MATERIALS

In order to translate a picture of a pattern into something you can use to cut and sew your quilt, you'll need a few basic supplies. Pencils, paper, cardboard, and rulers are probably already available to you. Patterns can be made with equipment no more specialized than this. However, there are a few things that will make the process easier.

- **Graph paper:** Most patterns are pictured on a grid. The chore of translating that to the size you want for your quilt is much easier with commercial graph paper. Marking a grid yourself can be tedious and, if you're not accurate, your pattern won't be either. Graph paper can also be helpful if you're designing your own quilt. Shading light and dark squares to try different variations of a geometric design can save you time later.

- **Template material:** For more complex patterns, most quilters either make templates out of cardboard or use commercial plastic templates. Keep in mind that, if you're cutting several pieces from the same pattern, cardboard will begin to wear down and your last pieces will be slightly smaller than the first. Plastic templates are clear so, when you lay it on your fabric to mark it, you can see exactly what your cut piece will look like. Cardboard, however, won't melt as plastic will if you use your template as a pressing guide to turn under seam allowances. It may shrink slightly but it won't be enough to matter unless you're making a great many identical pieces. The solution is to make several cardboard templates of each size.

## MARKING TOOLS

At several points in the process of making your quilt, you'll need to mark lines or designs on your fabric. You won't want any of these marks to show on the finished quilt, yet they need to remain long enough for you to use them effectively.

Unlike dressmaking, where you pin your pattern to the fabric and then cut around it, when you cut your quilt pieces, you'll be drawing around your pattern, then cutting them out. A hard lead pencil is often used for this purpose. A soft lead pencil will smear and make your thread dirty. It's recommended you use an art gum eraser or an eraser made especially for fabric to get rid of any lines that show after stitching rather than counting on them to come out in the wash.

There are also special quilt pencils that may be a little safer and they come in different colors to ensure they'll show up on any type of fabric. Many quilters love architects' silver pencils because their marks show up on nearly everything. Just don't iron over the marks as this will set them onto the fabric.

Tailor's chalk can also be used but it doesn't make a very fine line and often rubs off before you're ready. It is handy, however, for quick-fix marking while you're quilting if a line isn't showing up sufficiently or if you've decided to add an extra one. Keep it sharp with an emery board.

Once all the pieces of your quilt are cut and sewn together, you'll need to mark out a quilting design. This is your guide to the quilting itself. The simplest method is to use commercial stencils available in quilt shops and catalogs. Draw the design onto your quilt cover through the slits in the stencil with your quilting pencils or a regular hard lead pencil.

Another method is to use dressmakers' tracing paper as if it were carbon paper and draw over the design. Tracing paper comes in a variety of colors to show up on different colors of fabric. It should wash out of any fabric you'd be using for quilts. If you're tracing the same design several times, be sure to make more than one copy as continual tracing will eventually wear through the paper.

Before these supplies were available, tailor's chalk was rubbed over a paper pattern that had been pricked at intervals with a pin and would be brushed off when the quilt was done. Unfortunately, with all the handling and rolling of the quilt as it's stitched, the chalk might brush off too soon.

## HOOPS OR FRAMES

You will need to be able to hold your quilt in place while you stitch the layers together. While it's possible to quilt a small project without any kind of hoop or frame, your stitches will be more even and the result smoother if you use one or the other.

Since it takes both hands to quilt, something that holds the quilt for you is helpful for even the smallest of projects but is a necessity for large ones.

- **Hoops:** Embroidery hoops come in many sizes and the heavier ones can accommodate the layers of a quilt. A small project might be worked on one of these. There are sturdier quilting hoops the size of embroidery hoops that have an interlocking feature to keep the thickness of your quilt layers from causing the outside hoop to pop off.
- **Frames:** The standard quilt frame is designed to accommodate any size quilt. The whole width of the quilt is available to the quilter at once and the ends that are finished or waiting to be worked can be rolled out of the way.

Modern quilting frames can be tipped for more comfortable sewing or set level for group quilting. Their biggest disadvantage is they take up about as much room as a piano (though they are easier to move) and not every home can accommodate one.

## SEWING MACHINES

While not absolutely necessary, the modern sewing machine can be a very useful tool for quilting. Piecing is not only faster and straighter when done on a machine but also stronger. If you have a sewing machine, make sure it's clean and in good working order before attempting to quilt with it and replace the needle with a new one to avoid skipped stitches. A feeder foot or walking foot would be a good investment to ensure all three layers move along under the needle at the same rate.

## Choosing and Handling Fabric

The fabric will be a major factor in the appearance and durability of your finished quilt. The wrong fabric can cause frustration during construction and even disappointment when the sewing is done. Knowing what to look for and what to avoid at the fabric store can make all the difference.

### FABRIC TERMS

Don't be confused by the terms you hear tossed about in the fabric store. Here are a few of the most common ones to help you start speaking the language:

- **Yard goods** refers to fabrics sold by the yard or fraction of a yard.
- The tightly woven finished sides of a length of fabric are called the **selvage**.
- The threads that run from selvage to selvage are called **crosswise threads**, with **lengthwise threads** running, of course, the length of the fabric.

- **Bias** refers to an imaginary line in the fabric on the diagonal with these threads.
- The seemingly miles of fabric wrapped around a cardboard core and displayed in a store is called a **bolt**. Fabric can be anywhere from 36" to 60" wide (measured selvage to selvage) but most cotton fabrics suitable for quilting are between 42" and 45".
- **A fat quarter**, a quilter's favorite, is a half-yard of fabric cut in half lengthwise. In other words, it's a piece approximately 18" × 22". A normal (skinny) quarter would be 9" by around 44". Fabric stores cut and fold them into attractive little squares for quilters because they're a handy size.
- **Broadcloth** refers to a plain-weave fabric with a semiglossy finish. Most quilting fabric is broadcloth or broadcloth weight.

## COTTONS AND BLENDS

Cotton has been the preferred fabric for quilt making for around three hundred years. It is colorfast, washable, easy to work with, and durable. Its only close rivals are today's cotton-polyester blends. An old-fashioned quilt pattern done all in cotton resembles an antique quilt because of the traditional fabric. Cotton is soft to the touch and the preferred material for baby quilts. Pure cotton creases easily, which can mean a great deal when you're turning under a raw edge on a small piece for appliqué.

On the other hand, cotton-polyester quilts will keep that brand-new look longer. It's the polyester that gives the blended fabrics their permanent-press quality, making them look smooth and crisp. The colors will be a bit brighter and slower to fade than those in 100 percent cotton. Some quilters say 30 percent polyester should be the maximum, but 60/40 cotton-polyester blends are common and used often.

## MIXING BLENDS WITH PURE COTTON

A quilt should probably be made from only one type of fabric: all cotton or all blends that have as close to the same percentage of cotton as possible. This is especially true if the quilt is made up of large pieces. However, it won't be disastrous to do a little mixing. The smaller the pieces in the quilt, the less the differences in the fabrics will show.

Fabric bought in remnant bins, at garage sales, and even scraps left over from your own sewing may keep their exact content a secret. A clue will be how wrinkled they are after being washed. The more they wrinkle, the higher the cotton content. If you must know if two or more fabrics are of similar content, carefully burn small equal-sized pieces in heatproof dishes and compare the ash. Polyester will melt, rather than burn, and leave tiny beads behind.

## SOLIDS AND PRINTS

Now that you know what types of fabrics to look for, you're ready to make your selections. As far as color choices go, there are two basic types of quilts: scrap quilts that use up lots of leftover fabric and quilts in which all the fabric pieces coordinate with one another.

For scrap quilts, the more variety in color and texture the better. In fact, in charm quilts, no two pieces should be from the same fabric. All you have to consider is the placement of the pieces, trying not to put pieces of similar color or similarly sized prints next to each other.

For the color-coordinated quilt, your tastes will be your best guide, but consider a few suggestions. Before you go shopping, cut a window in a piece of cardboard the size and shape of the primary pieces of your quilt. As you look at fabrics, test how the print appears in the window. You don't want a fabric where the motif is too large for the piece or one where the pictures are so far apart it would be possible to cut a piece and miss the picture entirely.

## FABRIC FOR BACKING

The fabric for the quilt backing is as important as the cover. Most of the same rules apply because it will be quilted along with the cover and will ultimately receive the same care. Unbleached muslin is a traditional quilt backing. It is often sold in widths up to 108". Special quilt backing, sometimes called sheeting, is sold in some fabric stores. It can be as wide as 112" and can eliminate the necessity of piecing the back to fit even a king-sized bed.

## TYPES OF BATTING

The last component of your quilt is the batting. Commercial batting is generally polyester but cotton batting might be available in some specialty stores. Quilt batting is folded and rolled very tightly to fit into the plastic bag it comes in. A day or so before you're ready to assemble your quilt, unroll the batting and lay it flat. Smooth the wrinkles gently with your hand. A light misting with water will help the worst of the wrinkles disappear.

## Preparing New Fabric

Once you've chosen the fabric to use in your quilt, the hard part is over, but you aren't quite ready for quilting. New fabric needs some preparation before it's ready to be cut for your quilt. A little extra work now can save considerable grief later.

*Because all new fabric frays in the wash, a load made up entirely of new fabric pieces can become a tangled mess. Therefore, it's better to toss a length or two in with a regular load of laundry. Clipping the selvage corners will also help minimize tangling but will put more loose threads in your washer. Untangle the pieces and cut away the loose threads before you put the pieces in the dryer.*

### PRESHRINKING YOUR FABRIC

Cotton shrinks more than cotton-polyester blends do and some cottons shrink more than others. You want the fabrics you've chosen for your quilt to do all their shrinking before they're pieced together. To do this, simply launder them the way you would the quilt. The gentle cycle and cold water are probably fine for most quilts but a baby quilt might need a hot water wash at some point in its life. If your fabric can't handle that, it's best to find out now.

## STRAIGHTENING YOUR FABRIC

Most fabric is not exactly straight with the grain when you buy it, meaning the lengthwise threads are not exactly perpendicular to the crosswise threads. If you don't correct this, your quilt won't be straight either.

To see if your fabric is straight with the grain, pull a thread near one raw edge until it breaks and cut along the line you've created. Repeat this until you've cut from one selvaged edge to the other. Fold this newly cut edge in half and hold the fabric up to see if the selvages hang in a straight line. If they don't, your fabric should be straightened.

Fabric is straightened by pulling on the bias to force the lengthwise and crosswise threads into alignment. Stretch the entire surface of the fabric, not just across the center. And remember, unless the fabric has the same length and width, corner to corner is not the true bias. Stretch several places along the bias and test again.

## Simple Wall Hanging Project

The quilting stitch, while time consuming, is not particularly difficult. It does take some practice, however. If you practice on a small wall hanging, you'll have fun and wind up with something worth keeping when you're done. This simple wall hanging uses picture print fabric so there's no piecing or appliqué to do. An inexpensive embroidery hoop serves as the frame and hides the raw edges at the same time.

## SUPPLIES YOU WILL NEED
You'll need the following things to complete this project.

### Picture Print Fabric
You'll need a piece of printed fabric with a picture at least 3" or 4" across. An equal radius of neutral color surrounding the picture is ideal. Fabrics printed to look like patchwork quilts, sometimes called cheater's quilting, often have large picture "blocks" that work well for this project.

### Embroidery and Quilting Hoops
You will need an inexpensive embroidery hoop to use as a permanent frame for your mini-quilt. Embroidery hoops can easily be found in sizes anywhere from 3" to 14" in diameter. Choose one of appropriate size to frame the picture you've chosen. The best way to do this is to have your fabric with you when you pick out the hoop.

You'll also need a good-quality quilting hoop for the actual stitching. For lap quilting (i.e., quilting without a freestanding frame or hoop), a hoop of about 8" in diameter is a convenient size.

If your picture will be smaller than that, you may be able to do your quilting in the same hoop you'll use later for framing. Or you can enlarge the project by basting strips of fabric along each side. These extensions will fit into the quilt frame and hold the work in place.

*Don't be confused into thinking lap quilting means quilting with no hoop at all. It's possible to quilt this way but, without stretching the quilt out flat in a hoop, your stitches will be too tight and your finished quilt will be puckery.*

### Ruffle

If it seems appropriate to your picture, you may want to put a ruffle around your wall hanging. A length of commercial ruffle a couple inches longer than the circumference of the hoop or frame will be sufficient.

Ruffles are available in many colors, sizes, and styles. Again, it's best to have your fabric with you when you shop for the trim. Be sure the ruffle is stiff enough that it'll stand out around the hoop.

### Other Supplies

The other supplies you'll need for this project are:

- Quilt batting
- Backing fabric
- Quilting thread

- Basting thread
- Needles and pins
- A thimble
- Liquid or hot glue

## ASSEMBLING YOUR QUILT

Now that you have all your materials, it's time to put together your mini-quilt.

### Cut

Cut the printed fabric in a square 2" or 3" larger than the hoop frame you've chosen. This is now the cover of your miniature quilt.

Place your cover right side up on the quilt batting and smooth both layers out with your hands. Cut the batting slightly larger than the cover. Place both layers on the wrong side of the backing fabric and cut around it as well, making it the same size as the batting. If these layers were cut exactly the same size as the cover, they'd have to be placed exactly on top of one another to ensure there is batting and backing behind all edges of the cover.

### Baste

Pin the layers together, checking the back to be sure it's as smooth as the front. A pin every 2" or 3" will be enough.

With a contrasting thread, baste the layers together. Knot the thread and begin in the center with a running stitch. To do a running stitch, weave the needle in and out of the fabric several times before you pull it all the way through. These stitches can be ½" long or longer and don't have to be pretty since you'll be removing them as you quilt. Stitch to one corner and cut the thread. Repeat for the other corners, always beginning in the center.

If your hanging is more than 6" or 7" across, you could run stitches from near the center to the sides and to the top and bottom as well. The purpose of basting is to hold the layers securely so nothing shifts while you quilt.

### The Quilting Stitch

The ideal quilting stitches are straight, even stitches through the layers of the quilt that look the same on the back as the front. Expert quilters take as many as ten or twelve stitches per inch. Beginners should be happy with eight.

For this project, you'll begin by quilting along the outline of your picture. Follow these steps and practice making stitches that are as tiny and even as possible. A few lines of stitching inside the picture can be very effective but don't try to outline every detail. Think in terms of foreground and background and outline a few key areas.

### Bury the Knot

Thread an 18" length of quilting thread onto a between needle. Tie a simple knot in the thread close to one end. Along the stitching line and about 1" away from where you want to begin stitching, insert the needle through the top layer of the fabric only and out at the point where you'll begin stitching.

Pull the needle through and gently tug the knot through the cover so it'll be hidden in the batting. Sometimes scratching it with your thumbnail will encourage it through the cloth. If you're having trouble, you might use the tip of the needle to lift the fabric near the knot and pull it over the knot as you tug on the thread.

Be sure to enter the thread on the line where you'll be stitching. This prevents the shadow of the knot or any tail behind it from showing as it might if you bury the knot outside the stitching line. This is especially important if you're using colored thread.

### Downward Stitch

With the index finger of your nondominant hand under your work at the point where you'll begin stitching, balance the frame against your body. Insert the tip of the needle about 1/16" from the exit point of the thread. Use your index finger to stop the needle as soon as it emerges from the quilt.

**Figure 7-1:** *A cutaway view of the quilt during the first downward stitch*

Upward Stitch

Gently place your thimble-protected middle finger on the eye end of the needle and rock the needle to the side until it's nearly lying on the surface of the quilt. Push up with your finger under the quilt. At the same time, push down on the top of the quilt with your thumb, just ahead of the needle. This makes it possible for the needle to get into a position nearly perpendicular to the part of the quilt it's going to enter.

The index finger under the quilt pushes the needle through the layers and the thumb stops it as it emerges. The thumb is the key to tiny stitches on top and the index finger is the key to tiny stitches on the bottom.

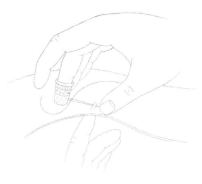

Figure 7-2: *A cutaway view of the quilt during the first upward stitch*

When the tip of the needle comes through the fabric and is stopped by the thumb, relax your thumb and rock the needle upward again, forcing the tip back through the layers. Your hand should look like Figure 7-1 again except there'll be a stitch on the needle (see Figure 7-2).

### Running Stitch

At first, you might want to push the needle through the cloth after only one or two stitches. Practice making tiny stitches initially, then see how many stitches you can get on a needle before you have to pull it through. There is a limit to how many stitches will work before you need to use pliers to get the needle through all the layers, but four or five stitches on the needle will help ensure your stitching is straight.

### Tying Off

When the thread is getting short enough to cause difficulty, it's time to tie it off and begin with another length of thread. While the thread is still on the needle, tie a knot in the thread about ¼" to ½" from the surface of the quilt. If you poke the end of the needle in the loop as you tighten the knot, you can guide the knot to end where you want it to.

Run the needle into the top layer of fabric at the point where it emerged and out again about 1" away. Be sure you do this along a stitching line. Pull until the knot has gone through the fabric and is in the batting layer. Tug the thread a little and clip it near the cloth. The knot and tail will be buried inside the quilt.

### Echo Stitching

Once you've gone all the way around the picture on your quilt, try echo stitching to get in some more practice. Echo stitches are rows of stitches running parallel to a design, mimicking its curves and angles. Think of it like ripples on the surface of a pond.

To judge where to run the row of echo stitches, use a ruler and hard lead pencil to mark a few spots ¼" from the finished row. A dot every 1" or so should be enough to guide you around the picture again. Continue the echo rows until you've filled the entire area that will be visible when the picture is centered in the hoop.

*Your fingers are bound to be tender after the first few times you quilt. The thumb and index finger that guide and pull the needle are especially vulnerable to soreness. Wrap the sore fingers in paper tape or adhesive bandages when you quilt until they heal enough to toughen up a bit. Soaking your hands in warm water after a quilting session can ease the soreness.*

## Finishing Touches

First, be sure to remove any remaining basting stitches. Erase any visible pencil marks. If your work seems smudged by your pencil marks or prolonged handling, you may want to wash it.

Your quilt will seem surprisingly puckered after being quilted and washed. Be certain all the pencil marks are gone, then iron it. Ironing a finished quilt isn't usually recommended because it flattens the batting; however, this project will look better on your wall if it's ironed. Stretch it out as you go so you don't iron puckers or creases in the unquilted areas.

### Framing the Quilt

Center your miniature quilt over the inside hoop of the embroidery hoop frame. Loosen the outside hoop and center the adjustable screw at the top of the picture. You'll be hanging the finished quilt from this screw.

Push the outside hoop down over the inside hoop, adjusting the quilt so it stays centered. Tighten the screw a little at a time, pulling the ends of the quilt tight as you go. When the quilt is centered but before the screw is completely tight, ease the outside hoop off a fraction. Run a few drops of glue between the exposed inner hoop and the quilt and along the line between the back of the outside hoop and the quilt. Slide the hoop back in place and tighten thoroughly, making any necessary last-minute adjustments. Allow the glue to dry. Next, trim off the excess fabric flush with the back of the hoop frame.

### Adding the Ruffle

Trim the raw edge at one end of the ruffle. Press and stitch under a narrow hem. Use the ruffle to measure around the hoop frame to find where to put the second hem. Starting with the hemmed edge at the center top, lay it out carefully around the hoop. You'll be gluing the base of the ruffle against the raw edge of the quilt and the back of the hoop. Ideally, the gathering stitches of the ruffle should be hidden behind the hoop frame.

**Figure 7-3:** *The back view of the mini-quilt during the finishing steps*

Find the point where the ends of the ruffle will meet, allow for the hem, and trim and hem the second end. Glue the ruffle in place. If you're using liquid glue, you might need to push an occasional pin through the ruffle into the edge of the quilt to hold the ruffle in place until the glue dries. Inserting the pins at a sharp angle will be most effective. Let the glue dry, then hang your first quilt on the wall to enjoy!

## Nine-Patch Throw Quilt Project

Once you've gotten the hang of the mini-quilt, try this more advanced project. This makes a wonderful gift or an excellent lap robe or throw. Note the directions for this quilt are for machine piecing. However, if you don't have a machine, you can, of course, stitch the pieces by hand.

### FABRIC REQUIREMENTS

Nine-patch refers to a pattern of nine squares, generally of only two colors, which alternate in three rows of three. The nine square blocks are framed with panels of a coordinating fabric to keep the blocks from blending into one huge checkerboard. This 36" × 52" quilt calls for six blocks made of nine 4" (finished size) patches, separated and framed by 4" panels.

## AMOUNTS OF FABRICS

The yardages that follow assume the fabric you're buying is about 42" wide. If the width of the fabric is significantly different, adjust the yardages accordingly. And remember, it's better to have too much than too little. (You can always start your stash of scraps for future projects.) You will need:

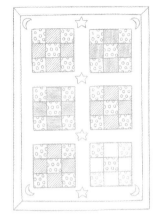

**Figure 7-4:** *The layout of a nine-patch quilt*

- 1 yard of a primary print for panel and border pieces
- ⅔ yard of a secondary print
- ⅙ yard each of six solid-color fabrics that coordinate with the prints
- 1⅔ yards for backing
- Piece of batting at least 38" × 54"
- 10 yards of yarn or crochet cotton for ties
- A sharp tapestry needle or large embroidery needle

You should be able to cut the thirty secondary-color patches from exactly ½ yard of fabric. If you're using the primary print fabric for the backing, 2½ yards should be sufficient for the panels, borders, and backing. One yard of the secondary fabric should be enough if you want to use it for the backing as well as the thirty patches. Cut the backing piece first and cut the smaller blocks or panels from what's left.

## Cut and Arrange the Pieces

Since all the pieces are squares or rectangles, there's no need to make templates. Be sure to iron the fabric first so your measurements will be accurate.

The patches on the finished quilt will be 4" × 4". Allowing ¼" all around for the seams, each patch will need to be cut 4½" square. Measure 4½" from the cut edge of your fabric and pull another thread or cut with a rotary cutter. If you're using a rotary cutter, you can fold the fabric and cut through as many as four layers at once if you're careful about keeping the edges lined up. Remember to cut away the selvage before cutting your strip into 4½" squares.

### The Patches

You will need thirty squares of the primary color and four of each of the six solid colors. But here's the fun of the nine-patch: If you discover you're short on the print fabric, use it for four patches per block instead of five and cut one more of each of the solid-color fabrics. Or, if you have a lot of scraps of juvenile prints, use a different print for the patches in each block. You could pick a different solid color to go with each print or choose one that goes well with them all.

### Panels and Borders

You will need to cut the border and panel pieces 4½" wide. You will need nine pieces that are 12½" long to fit vertically between and on either side of the blocks and four pieces that are 36½" long to run horizontally above, between, and below the rows of blocks.

Cut the fabric into seven strips, each 4½" wide. Four of these strips will be used for the horizontal panels and borders, the other three will become the vertical panels and borders. Trim away the selvages but there's no need to cut the strips to their exact length. You can save time by doing that as you sew.

### Backing and Batting

The finished cover will be slightly less than 36" × 52". Your backing and batting will both need to be cut a couple inches larger than this. Pull a thread to cut the edge with the grain. Fold the cut edge in half, selvage to selvage. Pull on the diagonal until the selvages hang evenly.

### Three Patches Equal a Row

Begin with two patches that will be next to each other in a block. With right sides together, line up the edges and stitch ¼" from the raw edge. Being sure to keep track of which patch should be in the middle of the row, stitch a third patch to the first two. Set this row aside and repeat the process with each row of patches. You should have eighteen rows.

If all your blocks are the same, you can sew 4½" strips of fabric together in the order the blocks should be arranged in the top and bottom rows. Cut the connected strips into 4½" units. Do the same with strips arranged for the middle row. This can save considerable time if you're making a full-sized quilt.

Press the seam allowances toward the darker fabric. This ensures the allowance won't show through the front of the cover.

## Matching Seams

Group the pressed three-square units together by block again. With right sides together, line up the edges and seams. To be sure the seams match, pin the strips together exactly on the seam line. The seam allowances should be pressed to stagger rather than overlap, minimizing the bulk. You won't be sewing through more than four layers of cloth when you stitch the strips together. This also makes it easier to line up the seams.

Run a pin in and back out along the stitching line of the unit you've placed on top. Check the bottom unit. Does the part of the pin that's visible line up exactly with the stitching? If not, make the necessary adjustments.

When both seams are matched, check the fabric between the pins. Is it lying flat naturally? You need to be able to stitch without gathering or stretching one patch to fit the other. If you can't, you need to redo a seam. Use another unit to help you determine which seam is the culprit. It's easier to make a piece smaller than larger, but don't automatically solve the problem that way. Your finished block might end up a different size than the rest of the blocks and your problems will have increased considerably.

## Three Rows Equal a Block

When the seams line up, stitch the units together ¼" from the edge and repeat the process with the third row of patches. Set the new block aside and make the other five blocks the same way.

Press the seams. The direction isn't going to make a great deal of difference because, whichever way you choose, you'll be pressing darker allowances toward lighter fabric about half the time. An alternative would be to press the seams open but this is a little more time consuming. If you have a great deal of contrast between the hue of the fabrics in your quilt, it might be worth the extra effort, otherwise consistency is probably more important than which direction you choose.

Unless your blocks are all the same, you'll need to decide their placement on the finished quilt. Lay them out on a large surface such as the floor. You can spread your panel/border strips between them to get a better idea of what your quilt will look like. Switch the blocks around until you're satisfied.

Once you've made your decision, stack your blocks in order, bottom row blocks, middle, then top row. Left and right won't make any difference at this point unless you've used one-way fabric, in which case you'll need to keep careful track of what you're doing.

### Set the Quilt

Spread three of the panel strips across your lap. With right sides together, sew a panel strip to one side of the first block. You won't need to pin since there are no seams to match. Simply line up the edges and sew. When you come to the end of the block, cut the thread and trim the strip using the block as a guide.

Repeat the process with the other end of the block. Sew the second block in the stack to the panel you've just trimmed, then sew a third panel to the other end of it. You now have a completed row of your quilt.

Set this aside to press and repeat the process with the rest of the blocks. Iron the seams toward the panels and lay them out to recreate your chosen layout. Return to the sewing machine (if you're using one) and spread the remaining four panel strips across your lap. Sew the strips and rows of blocks together, trimming the excess from the panel strips at the end of each row. Press the seams toward the panels and your quilt cover is finished.

### Easy Assembly Method

This method of assembling a quilt works well with small projects. The idea is to sew the cover and back together with the right sides of the fabrics facing each other, a little like a pillowcase, then turn it right-side out. This saves the need for any form of binding or hemming of the edges of the quilt.

### Backing and Batting

Spread the batting out on the floor or other large surface. Smooth out any wrinkles. Spread the backing piece over it right-side up and pin them together in a few places. Baste the pieces together loosely and remove the pins. You won't need a great many basting stitches to hold these together for the next step.

### Assemble

Spread the cover right-side down on top of the backing. Carefully smooth out any wrinkles. Place a pin every few inches around the outside edge. The edges of the backing and batting should extend beyond the edge of the cover.

Stitch a ¼" seam around the outside edge of the cover, leaving only 10"–12" open on one side of the quilt. You'll need to stitch the backing to the batting at the opening. Move the cover out of your way and stitch along what would have been the stitching line, coming as close as possible to where the cover is stitched down without catching the cover in these stitches.

*You will want to sew with the batting down and the underside of the cover facing you. When you stitch the corners, take a stitch or two on the diagonal instead of making a sharp turn. This allows you to trim off more of the excess fabric and actually makes a sharper corner on the finished quilt.*

### Trim and Turn

Trim the backing to about 1/16" outside the cover's edge. The finished edge will lie smoother after it's turned if the two fabrics in the seam allowance are of different widths. Trim the batting close to the stitching and clip the four corners almost to the diagonal stitches.

Turn the quilt right-side out through the opening you left. Poke the corners out using a blunt object like the eraser end of a pencil. Never use a sharp object as you can easily rip open the seam or poke a hole in the fabric.

Press around the edge of the quilt, being careful to open the seam out as much as possible. Rolling the seam between your fingers can help with this. Turn the edges under in the opening and press them flat. Remove the basting stitches from the backing.

### The Blind Stitch

You need to close up the opening you left to turn the quilt but you want it to look as much like the machine stitches as possible. If done correctly, the blind stitch is nearly invisible.

Refer to Figure 7-5 and follow these steps.

1. Knot an appropriate length of the same thread you used to stitch around the quilt.
2. Bury the knot in the seam allowance, bringing the needle out at the end of the machine stitching.
3. Holding the layers between the thumb and forefinger of your nondominant hand, take a tiny stitch exactly on the crease of the cover.

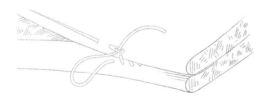

**Figure 7-5:** *The blind stitch*

4. Insert the needle in the backing even with where the needle left the cover and take another tiny stitch.

5. Repeat with another tiny stitch in the cover beginning exactly across from the end of the last stitch. The trick is to do all your forward movement with the thread inside the folds of cloth and not in the space between the layers.

### Tie the Quilt

The only thing left to do is secure the layers together. This quilt is going to be tied at the corners of every patch. This spaces ties evenly over the entire surface of the quilt at intervals close enough together to hold the batting in place.

### Baste

Spread out the quilt on a flat surface and smooth it out. Begin in the middle and pin the layers together every 6" to 8". Flip the quilt over to be sure the backing is as smooth as the front. Move pins if necessary.

Since this is a relatively small project, pin basting will be sufficient while you tie. However, if you're reluctant to get a few scratches from the pins as you work, baste the layers together, beginning in the center and working outward the same way you basted the mini-quilt. Knot your contrasting thread and work a running stitch from the center to each corner, then from the center to each side.

## Yarn for Tying

Cotton or acrylic yarn is recommended for tying. Some quilters use wool because it shrinks and frizzes into tight little knots when the quilt is washed and there's no danger of the ties coming out. There's also no danger of anyone lying on the quilt because those knots are as hard as buttons. Acrylic and cotton ties will last well enough and, if done correctly, won't come out anyway.

The color you choose for the ties will depend on whether you want the ties to decorate the surface of your quilt or blend to near invisibility. There's no rule that says the ties must all be the same color, either. Consider how your yarn looks with all the different fabrics before you make your decision.

## The Tie Stitch

There is no need to cut a length of yarn from the skein. Simply thread the loose end of it onto your sharp tapestry or embroidery needle. The smallest needle available that will still allow the yarn to go through the eye will be easiest to draw through the layers of your quilt.

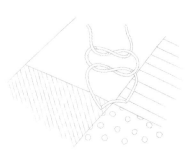

Beginning near the center of your quilt, insert the needle about ⅛" diagonally from the corner of a patch and out again ⅛" on the other side. Draw about 4" of yarn through the quilt. Take a second stitch back through the same holes.

**Figure 7-6:** *Double stitch and double knot to tie*

Tie the yarn in a double knot and trim to about ¾" or whatever length you desire.

With the thumb and forefinger of your nondominant hand, untwist the yarn slightly. Stick the needle in the yarn just above the knot and run it outward to fray the yarn. This will decrease the chances of the knots coming untied.

Rethread the needle and repeat across the surface of the quilt, working outward from the center. Sometimes it's easier to catch any skipped sites by checking the back of the quilt. The little loops of yarn should be evenly spaced over the entire surface.

Sometimes ties are tied in bows instead of frayed. This can be very pretty but isn't recommended for baby quilts as tiny fingers can catch in the loops. However, it might work well on the living room throw.

## Signing Your Work

Any work of art deserves to carry the artist's signature. Your quilted wall hangings, especially ones that express your special interests or milestones, should be signed. Nearly all quilters put their names on their quilts. Most also include the date or at least the year. Some record the date the quilt was begun as well as the date it was finished, and many include their maiden name to help future genealogists.

There are many quilters who include the quilt's name and sometimes more information about the pattern. Some quilters put their name and whatever other information they want to include on a piece of cloth and stitch it to the quilt while others sign directly on it. Most quilters put their names on the back of their work, this way the information is on the quilt forever but doesn't detract from its appearance.

Generally, if a quilter puts her name on the front, she'll try to make it less conspicuous. Some will use quilting thread to sew their names in tiny stitches taken only through the cover of the quilt and a few will even work their names into the stitching pattern.

You can sign your quilt with ink or a permanent marker, or sign it in pencil and stitch over the lines. Cursive letters are easier than printed letters because they're joined. A single strand of embroidery thread works best for the stitching. Use a simple backstitch, sometimes called a stem stitch.

If you decide to sign in ink, iron over it to set it. Covering the signature with a cloth dipped in vinegar and water and then wrung out and ironing over that is even better—you don't want the ink to run when the quilt is washed. If you're signing a piece of cloth to appliqué to the quilt, backing it with iron-on interfacing or butcher paper first makes it easier to sign. Remove the paper before sewing it to the quilt.

**CHAPTER 8**

# SOAPMAKING

People have made their own soaps for centuries but, in recent times, soapmaking has become somewhat of a lost art. Instead, people buy manufactured soap with numerous commercial dyes and fragrances, many of which aren't good for the skin. Making your own soap is not only creative and fun, it's actually easy to do once you get down some basic safety guidelines. Using the advice and recipes in this chapter, you'll be able to make your own soaps for yourself or to give as gifts. The best part is you'll know exactly what's in your soap and exactly what you're putting onto your body—what could be more comforting than that?!

## Soapmaking Safety Gear

In any new crafting endeavor, taking the time to obtain the proper equipment makes everything else go smoothly. This is especially important in soapmaking where you're working with heat and caustic chemicals. If you fear you can't sufficiently control your surroundings to keep and use soapmaking materials safely, do not make soap at home. However, soap is made without incident every day by thousands of people. By following instructions and using safety gear, you'll be able to relax and enjoy the soapmaking process.

## EYE PROTECTION

Make sure the eye protection you use is resistant to impact, caustics, and heat. If you wear glasses, get goggles that are large enough to wear over them. The danger to your eyes comes from the potential of lye particles, lye solution, raw soap, hot oils, and other liquids splashing on your face. As long as you work mindfully, you'll experience few, if any, splashing events. However, you don't want to be caught unprotected in the event one occurs.

## GLOVES

Regular rubber kitchen gloves provide appropriate protection for your hands and lower arms. Make sure the gloves you buy have textured fingers so you can keep a firm grip on your equipment. Some soapmakers prefer heavy-duty gloves. Just be sure you can use your fingers freely.

When you're finished with your soapmaking project for the day, clean your gloves well with soap and water. If you clean and dry them, they'll last quite some time. Turn them inside out to dry and store them only after they've dried completely.

Be sure to protect your arms above the gloves with a long-sleeve shirt. An oversized button-up shirt with sleeves you can roll up is ideal.

## PAINTER'S PAPER DUST MASK OR FILTER MASK

Caustic steam will rise when you combine the lye and water. Usually it's enough just to stand back and not breathe the steam but, if you're concerned about sensitivity, take the extra precaution of wearing a painter's paper dust mask or filter mask over your mouth and nose.

*Like candle making and all other tasks involving a stove, hotplate, or other heat source, it's a good idea to keep a fire extinguisher within easy reach. Make sure your fire extinguisher is charged and ready to go. When you need a fire extinguisher is not the time to wonder where it is or if it's charged. Read the instructions ahead of time so you know how to use it.*

## VINEGAR

Vinegar has traditionally been used as a neutralizer for lye and raw soap spills but you shouldn't pour vinegar onto an alkaline spill on your skin. It's a good idea to let your doctor know you're making soap and to ask about the best way to handle skin contact with caustics. If you come into contact with lye or raw soap batter, gently wipe the spill from your skin, then flush the area with water. This is when you would douse the area with vinegar if desired. Flush again with water then wash with soap and water. Don't wait to finish stirring your batch before rinsing and neutralizing a smear of raw soap on your skin. Do it as soon as it gets on you.

## Equipment Needed

With careful research and shopping, you can outfit yourself for soapmaking for far less money than you might think. Use recommended equipment at first, then create your own system variations as you gain experience.

### SCALE

The best way to measure ingredients for making soap is by weight. Therefore, you'll need a good scale. Digital postal scales, available at office supply stores, are the choice of many soapers. They usually run on 9-volt batteries, have the tare feature, weigh objects in ¼-ounce increments, and can handle a maximum of 10 pounds. This set of specifications is sufficient for most home soapmakers.

### THERMOMETER

You'll need an instant-read thermometer. There are many instances in soapmaking where the accurate measurement of temperature is essential. You may want to get two in case you need to measure the temperatures of two containers at the same time.

## POTS AND PANS

When buying your soapmaking pots and pans, stainless steel is the way to go. You can find stainless steel pots and pans at extremely reasonable prices at restaurant supply, warehouse, discount, and thrift stores. You absolutely must not use nonstick, aluminum, cast iron, or tin. These materials are called reactive because they will react with the soaps, ruining both soap and pan. Don't even try "just to see." They will react badly, even violently and toxically, with the lye used in the soapmaking process.

## DOUBLE BOILER

Double boilers are used in many kinds of soapmaking. The basic 2-quart, 2-part stainless steel double boiler is perfect for the soap-casting recipes in this chapter. You can improvise a double boiler using a saucepan and a stainless steel mixing bowl that rests securely but not tightly on the pan. (Always be sure when using any kind of double boiler to not let it boil dry.)

## STAINLESS STEEL UTENSILS

Stainless steel stirring spoons, slotted spoons, potato mashers, and ladles are all very useful. You probably already have these in your kitchen and it's safe to use them for your first few batches. As long as you clean them thoroughly, there's no danger in using them afterward because the metal doesn't readily absorb or react with the soap. If you find yourself making a great deal of soap, however, it may be easier to invest in stainless steel tools just for soaping.

 *Some stainless steel tools are held together with reactive metal screws, bolts, or brads. You probably won't be able to tell what type of metal the fasteners are, so choose utensils that are all one piece or have "all stainless construction" printed on the package. If in doubt, pass it by.*

## SILICONE UTENSILS

Silicone rubber scrapers (or "spatulas") are useful tools. Choose a one-piece model so you'll never lose the scraper part in a batch of soap.

## MEASURING EQUIPMENT

The small-batch cold-process recipes in this book call for two 4-cup measures: one for mixing the lye solution and another for mixing the oils and stirring the soap. The measures are also used in some liquid, melt-and-pour, and hand-milling techniques. They are, of course, always useful for measuring water. It's tempting to use the attractive, thinner heatproof glass, but stick to the heavy-duty variety as the thin glass will shatter.

Sets of stainless steel measuring cups and spoons are used in nearly all techniques. It's best to steer clear of plastic measuring cups and spoons. While they can be good for some things, they may be corroded by essential and fragrance oils or marred by heat.

## SOAP MOLDS

Your first batches of soap will very probably be poured into "found" molds. Shoeboxes lined with plastic bags, baby-wipe containers, inexpensive plastic storage containers, and more have all been pressed into service as soap molds. You can use tubes from paper towels or toilet paper rolls. Empty plastic wrap and aluminum foil boxes make small, lidded molds. Beginning soapmakers don't need the latest in soap-mold technology. Your mold needs and desires will grow as you gain experience.

If you're using something plastic for a mold, such as a baby-wipe container, be sure to test it for heat resistance. Because of the high temperatures involved in soapmaking, you need plastics that won't collapse when exposed to hot soap. The easiest way to check a mold for heat safety is to place it in the sink and fill it with boiling water. If it melts, it obviously won't be useful. If it warps and distorts, it isn't a good choice either.

You may need some additional supplies to make it easier to get your soaps out of their molds. Soapmakers struggle with unmolding all the time. A simple way to ensure ease of release is to line the bottom and sides of the mold. You could lightly brush vegetable oil on the inside of the mold, then cut plastic sheeting, freezer paper, overhead projector transparencies, or other similar materials to size and press onto the oiled surface. Smooth out bumps and creases in the liner to ensure smooth surfaces on your soap. If all's gone as it should, all you'll have to do is turn the mold over and the beautiful soap will plop out onto your workspace. Remove the liner and clean it up for reuse.

### CUTTING TOOLS

The simplest soap cutter is a stainless steel table knife. Most soapers prefer non-serrated knives since they make a clean cut. However, soapmakers have adapted all kinds of tools into soap cutters. Dough scrapers borrowed from baking and putty knives and drywall tape spreaders borrowed from home improvement work very well.

## Techniques and Ingredients for Your First Batch of Soap

In this chapter, you'll learn how to make soap using the "cold process." Cold-process soapmaking is the basic form of hand-made, from-scratch soapmaking. It's called cold process because there's no cooking involved. Beyond heating the oils enough to liquefy them, there's no heat applied during the creation of the soap. You'll make luscious, gorgeous, gentle, bubbly soap with a fine texture via this process. The cold-process soapmaking technique is relatively simple and gets easier with practice. In short, a blend of oils is mixed with a simple solution of lye and water, stirred until thickened, then poured into a mold.

The transformation of oils into soap, called saponification, can only happen through the interaction of a lye solution with oils. Used carelessly, lye can cause severe burns and serious injury. It's impossible to overemphasize the necessity of smart safety practices when handling lye, lye solutions, and raw and "young" soap. This chapter will walk you through how to make lye soap safely at home.

## USING LYE

All soap is made with a caustic called lye. For the recipes in this chapter, you'll use a lye made of sodium hydroxide (chemical formula NaOH), which is used to make solid soap. Sodium hydroxide is easily available in 18-ounce plastic cans at grocery, hardware, and restaurant supply stores. It is generally stocked alongside the drain cleaners. Do not buy anything other than pure sodium hydroxide. There are other drain cleaners available but they include substances that are not at all suitable for soapmaking. You may also purchase sodium hydroxide from soapmaking suppliers.

Store your sodium hydroxide in a safe, dry place. The space under the kitchen sink is not a good idea, especially if you have kids. Many home soapers have a lye safe just for lye storage. Lye safes can range from a box in the garage clearly marked "Lye! Do Not Touch!" to a metal cabinet with locking doors.

You can make a practical, easy-to-create lye safe from a plastic storage box with a tight-fitting lid. Label it clearly and store it where you think it will be safest in your home. Storing your lye safe on a high shelf isn't recommended since you can easily drop it, especially if you keep more than a few pounds at home. Keeping it on the floor of a closet or garage will work.

In your lye safe, keep the plastic cans of lye in plastic bags. Label three bags: one for unopened cans, one for partially used cans, and one for empties. Take care in how you dispose of empty containers. Neutralize the lye dust by rinsing the containers with a vinegar-and-water solution. If you have a hazardous material drop-off day in your community, take your empty lye cans to the collection point.

## HOW DOES LYE MAKE SOAP?

In simplest terms, you combine lye, oils, and a liquid to make soap. The liquid may be water, milk, herbal infusions, or any liquid with a relatively neutral pH. Each liquid requires specific soapmaking techniques.

The purpose of liquid in lye soapmaking is to get the lye and oils together. In solution with water, lye molecules are more easily able to reach the molecules of oil. When they come into contact, the lye and oil molecules rearrange themselves and become soap and glycerin. If you were to simply add lye to oil without the liquid, the transformation process would be much different and you'd end up with a big, caustic mess.

The amount of lye used in a recipe depends on how much of each oil you use. Each oil has a saponification value, which is the amount of lye it takes to turn one ounce of oil into soap. Soap recipes are calculated to make sure they have the proper balance of oils, water, and lye.

## COMBINING LYE WITH WATER

An important step in soapmaking is combining lye with water. This creates an extremely violent, volatile chemical reaction. It is essential that you add lye to the water rather than water to the lye. Mixing these two components releases a great deal of energy in the form of heat immediately upon contact. If you pour cold water on top of lye, you could end up with a volcano-like eruption that would be extremely dangerous.

When you add water to lye, the chemical reaction causes the water and lye solution to heat to near-boiling temperatures almost immediately. A crust forms over the top of the lye, which seals in the reaction. The reaction of the lye and water proceeds normally but in a confined space, causing a buildup of heat energy that eventually bursts open like a bomb, showering the area with dangerously caustic material.

 *Always add lye to cold liquid. The reaction is so violent and rapid that, if you add lye to hot liquid, you'll be dangerously close to or over the boiling point in no time. Never add lye to hot liquid.*

Even when you correctly add lye to water, do so with care. When you add lye to the liquid, the solution will heat up very quickly and steam. Do not breathe the steam. Usually it's enough just to stand back and not breathe the steam, but if you're concerned about sensitivity to lye steam, wear a painter's paper dust mask or filter mask over your mouth and nose.

## LYE SOLUTION TEMPERATURE

The lye-and-water solution will heat up to about 180°F. You need to let the solution cool before combining it with the prepared oils. Soapmaking temperatures can range from room temperature (as long as the room is warm enough to keep the oils liquid) to as high as 120°F.

You can take the steaming lye solution outside to let it cool, just be sure it's in a safe place where no one can get to it and it won't get knocked over. It's also a good idea to cover the container so no leaves or other debris fall into it. The more surface area your lye container has, the faster it will cool. It's better to have an oversized pitcher than one that will be so deeply full it takes ages to cool. Leaving the lid off the pitcher will help with cooling. Be patient and monitor how long the cooling takes so you can plan for future batches.

There are some soapmakers who insist that the temperatures of the lye solution and the oil combination must be exactly the same and there are some who never even check the temperature. You should start learning your soapmaking techniques by following the temperature guides given in the recipes you're using. After a lot of experience with variations in temperatures and how those variations affect the process and the product, you can then make your own decisions about how to manage temperature.

## SAPONIFICATION

*Saponification* is an essential term of soapmaking vocabulary. Meaning "to turn into soap," it is what the reaction between the lye solution and the oils is called. Saponification starts as soon as the lye solution and oils come into contact with each other. The liquid, such as water or milk, facilitates the reaction by making sure all the various molecules come together.

The saponification process continues until all the lye and oils have reacted. In cold-process soapmaking, this can take a few weeks or more. As the soap ages, the reaction slows down considerably until eventually no unreacted alkali remains. "Young" soap will still have some alkalinity but this level decreases as the soap ages.

Alkalinity, and acidity as well, is measured on the pH scale. This scale is divided into a range of pH measures from 0 to 14. Substances with high pH factors, such as lye, are alkalis or bases, while those with low pH factors, like vinegar, are acids. Neutrals are found in the middle, around a pH of 7. Your soap should have a pH between 6 and 10.

A soap is said to be fully saponified when there is exactly enough oil and lye to fully react. Since you usually want a little extra oil in your soap for gentleness and as a moisturizer, most soaps are formulated with slightly more oil than will completely saponify.

## SUPERFATTING

*Superfatting* is also called a "lye discount." You can create a gentler soap by calculating a lye discount into your recipe. A lye discount is a reduction from the total amount of lye needed to completely saponify the oils. Another way to create a gentler soap is to superfat it by adding extra oils at the end of the stir before you pour. Overly lye-discounted or superfatted soap is softer and prone to rapid spoilage; however, lye-heavy soap is a worse problem as it makes harsh, caustic, and unusable soap.

The lye soap recipes in this chapter are created with a 5–7 percent lye discount and most contain one or more superfatting agents. If you want to add more superfatting agents, keep it to 1 tablespoon per pound of oils or you'll get soap that's soft and spoils more quickly. You may prefer to add the superfatting agent at the beginning and calculate it into the oils when you make your own formulas.

## TRACE

The term *trace* refers to the presence of traces of the soap mixture on the surface of the mass when some is taken up on your stirrer and dribbled back in. If the dribble makes no mark, your soap has not traced. When it leaves a little lump on the surface that sinks in quickly, it's beginning to trace.

A trace state is described as light to heavy. (A soap is said to have reached full trace when it's at the state desired to do what you need it to next.) When a soap mixture traces, it's reached a certain level of saponification. You add color, scent, and other materials at varying levels of trace. As you gain experience,

Figure 8-1: *Oils and lye just combined (note transparency)*

Figure 8-2: *Oils and lye just combined in small container*

Figure 8-3: *A medium trace*

you'll be able to recognize the signs of trace with no problem at all.

Because you'll be making 1-pound batches, your initial combination will probably look more like Figure 8-1.

When the oils and lye solution are first mixed together, the solution will be transparent. As you stir, it will become less so. Opacity and a slight graininess let you know your soap is tracing. There is also a subtle "soap smell" that comes at the same time. It isn't possible to describe it but you'll come to recognize and be reassured by it.

If you've made gravy or pancake batter, you've experienced the changing texture that many soapers compare to trace. A light trace may be like a thin pancake batter, a medium trace like a medium-thick gravy. If your soap gets gloppy, you've got a heavily traced batch and you need to get it into its mold as soon as possible.

Trace issues will cease to be issues as you make more and more soap. You must stir your soap to trace before pouring. If your soap hasn't traced, it will likely separate and remain unsaponified in layers of oils and lye solution.

## Adding Scent to Your Soap

When you pick up a bar of soap, the first thing you probably do is hold it to your nose and sniff. The packaging, color, and other visuals may attract you, but it's likely the scent that captures or repels you. Two of the easiest ways to scent your soap are to add essential oils or fragrance oils. When you create blends using both essential and fragrance oils, you need to be sure you use the proper measurements for each. Fragrance oil usage is usually about one-third the amount of essential oils. Not all fragrance oils are the same, so be sure you get the manufacturer's or distributor's rate of use for each oil you use.

### FRAGRANCE OILS

There are many sources of fragrance oils. For the purpose of soapmaking, a fragrance must be "soap safe." A soap-safe fragrance oil is formulated to react well with the various soapmaking processes. A fragrance that isn't soap safe for lye soapmaking can cause a soap batch to seize—become clumpy and hard as soon as it's added. It can also make soap separate, curdle, discolor, or streak. The scents may fade or mutate, making them unsuitable for soapmaking. Fragrance oils designed for cold-process soap hold up beautifully throughout the soapmaking process. It's important that you use soap-safe fragrance oils. These oils have been tested and selected by suppliers.

## ESSENTIAL OILS

In the study of soapmaking, one of the most interesting topics is essential oils. Unlike fragrance oils, which are mainly synthetic, essential oils are natural oils from plants. Like fragrance oils, essential oils contribute fragrance to your soap formulas but they may also add the health benefits of aromatherapy.

To enjoy the delights of essential oils, you must add a relatively large amount to the cold-process soap batter. The general usage rate is approximately ½ ounce of essential oils per 1 pound of base oils. (This varies when using absolutes, concretes, and resins.)

Both fragrance oils and essential oils are stirred into the soap batter after it has traced and before pouring it into your mold.

## Curing and Testing Your Soap

Curing refers to the period after cutting during which the soap becomes milder and harder—milder as saponification finishes and harder as water evaporates. You can extend the life of your soap through careful formulation and storage. Over time, exposure to heat and humidity can degrade the quality of your soaps. Soap that sits in water or is allowed to be in the stream of the shower will melt away rapidly, so dry it between uses. After cutting and while curing, soap needs to be kept at a relatively constant temperature and have good air circulation.

Depending on the amount of soap you make, you can dry your soap on a paper-covered cookie sheet or a small shelf, or create an entire curing and drying rack system. However you choose to cure it, be sure to turn it every few days during the first couple of weeks so it cures evenly.

## LYE SAFETY DURING CURING

Lye soap is made at home all the time in complete safety, but your safety depends on the use of common sense. If you plan well, everything will go smoothly. The more soap you make, the more you'll tailor your safety practices to your situation. Goggles and rubber gloves are safety essentials.

As mentioned earlier, lye is extremely caustic. When you first add lye to the liquid, the resulting solution is also extremely caustic. After this lye solution is mixed with the soapmaking oils, however, the soap begins to neutralize and becomes safe to touch after it has cured. Always wear goggles and rubber gloves when handling lye, lye solutions, raw soap, and fresh soap. If you're in doubt about how neutralized your soap is, err on the side of wearing goggles and gloves even when they're seemingly unneeded.

## TESTING FOR NEUTRALITY

You can test for neutrality in soap a number of ways. Using phenolphthalein or litmus papers is the most popular. Phenolphthalein is very reliable, inexpensive, and easy to use; you simply place a couple drops of the solution on the soap you're testing. If the solution turns pink, it's alkaline. If it stays clear, it's neutral. You can purchase litmus kits online and at your local garden center. Follow the directions on the kit (this often involves a color comparison chart on the box). You can also purchase an electronic pH meter. Soap is safe when it registers between 6 and 10 on the pH scale.

## CAUSTIC MESSES

While your soap is curing, test it every so often for neutrality. If your soap is more than two weeks old and is still highly caustic, something went wrong in the measurements. The soap should not be used. Find out from your city or county what the proper disposal method is for caustic materials.

Keep a caustic mess contained until you can dispose of it properly. Line a heavy cardboard box with two heavy plastic garbage bags, one inside the other. Fill the box with clay kitty litter deep enough to absorb the mess. Wearing goggles and gloves, pour or scrape the caustic mess into the bags. Add an equal measure of vinegar. If the mess is soupy, add more litter. Label the box and store it in a safe place until you dispose of it.

## EVAPORATION DURING CURING

Part of the curing process involves the evaporation of excess water from the bars. Ideally, there should be just enough liquid in the batch to ensure the success of the reaction between the lye and oils. A 4-ounce bar will lose approximately ¼ to ½ ounce of water this way. The bar will shrink a little from its original dimensions but should stay essentially the same.

## SOAP ASH

It is very common to find a thin layer of white powder on the top of your batch of soap. This is called "ash" and is harmless. It's essentially minerals from the water that have collected on the soap's surface. Using purified water is the main way to limit the formation of ash but even soap made with distilled water will sometimes have it. It can result from the composition of the lye or the way the ingredients worked together; sometimes there's no identifiable reason.

Placing plastic wrap on the surface of your poured soap is one way to eliminate the ash layer. Try to let the wrap cling to the surface on its own rather than pressing as you can add lumps and bumps to the surface if you push down too far. Peel it away when you're ready to unmold.

You can also remove the ash layer by hand when cutting your bars by using a cheese planer to cut away the ash. Some soapers set up their cutters to take off the layer during the cutting process while some just leave it. It isn't harmful and is an indication the soap was made by hand. It's ultimately an aesthetic choice.

 *If your soap has a crust of lye crystals, that is not ash. It is still caustic and you must handle it while wearing goggles and gloves. You may have added too much lye or stirred improperly, or the lye crystals may be the result of any number of other factors. The soap is probably lye-heavy and will never cure properly.*

## Cleaning Up

One of the many wonderful things about soapmaking is that, in many instances, it's a self-cleaning endeavor. After all, it's soap!

Make sure you don't rinse large blobs of gooey soap, either finished or unsaponified, down your drains. They'll clog up your drains almost immediately and take a lot of effort to clean out. Your best bet is to use smart cleanup techniques. Since the soap is caustic all the way through the process and for a few weeks after, always wear goggles and gloves while handling it, and keep track of all the utensils and equipment you've used with the lye.

After you've finished with a lye-touched tool, place it in the sink. If you add water, be sure not to hit it with a hard stream that will splatter. Keep adding the utensils as you finish, pouring vinegar on them as you go.

After you've scraped the last of the beautiful soap batter into the mold, wipe the inside of the pan and any other tools you've used. You can use paper towels but you'll go through a lot of them. A better idea is to get towels out of the rag bag and tear them into paper towel–sized soap cleanup towels. You can use your soap cleanup towels over and over, saving money and resources. Place the towels in a plastic bag for a day or two, then add them to the wash. The soap will have saponified enough for laundry use and will contribute to the cleansing.

*It's a good idea to clean up as you go. With lye soaps, use the kitchen sink to corral the lye-touched objects as you finish with them. Rinse the lye-pouring pitcher with water and a splash of vinegar, then fill it partway with water and more vinegar so you can place the other tools in a neutralizing bath.*

## Basic Cold-Process Soap

As a burgeoning soapmaker, you will find yourself always looking for ways to make better soap. The "rules" of soapmaking are different for everyone. As you gain experience with materials, processes, and procedures, you'll find ways to customize the basics to suit your own style (always keeping safety in mind). However, all journeys begin with a first step. Your first soapmaking experience should follow a simple, no-frills recipe.

For your first cold-process batch, here's an excellent 1-pound recipe. It will produce an unscented, uncolored soap. You should become familiar with this process before moving on to the fancier, scented soap recipes that follow. You'll notice the total weight comes to 24 ounces. It's called a 1-pound recipe because it uses 1 pound of oil.

For this batch, use two 4-cup glass measuring cups to make the lye solution, heat the oils, and blend the soap. (Note that, even when you're using measuring cups for mixing, you must always weigh your ingredients.) You'll use the first for the lye solution and the second for the oil mixture.

Remember to keep careful records of each batch of soap you make. This will help you keep track of what recipes you've used and where you are in your schedule for each batch. Later, when you explore variations on the basic recipes, taking thorough notes will help you keep track of what's working and what's not.

## BASIC COLD-PROCESS SOAP, 1-POUND RECIPE
You will need:

### Lye Solution
- 6 ounces water
- 2.25 ounces lye

### Base Oils
- 10 ounces olive oil
- 6 ounces coconut oil

### Superfat
- 1 tablespoon castor oil

### Directions
1. Put on all protective gear, including goggles, gloves, and long sleeves.
2. Place the water in a heatproof glass 4-cup measure. Sprinkle the lye slowly and carefully into the water. Stir until dissolved. Set the lye solution aside to cool.
3. In a second heatproof glass 4-cup measure, combine the olive oil, coconut oil, and castor oil. Melt in microwave or

over boiling water. (Coconut oil has a low melting point so it will melt quickly from an opaque white solid to a clear liquid.) As each setup is different, be sure to watch your microwave or double boiler closely, making note of how long it takes the mixture to melt. (Do not overheat as oils take longer to cool than the lye solution does.) Set the oils aside to cool.

4. When both mixtures are at 110°F, pour the lye solution in a thin stream into the oils. Stir constantly until the mixture traces, about 10–20 minutes. If using an immersion blender, it will take about a minute. (If using an immersion blender, take care not to whip air into the mixture.)

5. Once the soap batter traces, pour it into the mold, taking care to scrape all traced soap out of the cup.

6. Cover the mold with plastic wrap, then wrap the mold in a towel for warmth and let it sit for two days.

7. Wearing your goggles and gloves, try unmolding the soap by pulling out the sides and turning the mold upside down on a brown paper bag or paper towel on your work surface. Push on the bottom of the mold. If the soap doesn't readily release, place the mold in the freezer for 1 hour. Try again to remove it. It should easily release this time.

8. Using a stainless steel knife, cut the soap log into bars. Place them on a brown paper bag to dry. Turn them daily to ensure they dry evenly.

9. Your soap will be mild, quite firm, and ready to use in four weeks.
10. Store soap in a ventilated container.

This is your first batch of cold-processed lye soap! Congratulations! When you take it to the tub or shower, observe the smell, texture, lather, and rinsability. Although every bath with your own soap is a learning experience, be sure to take time to delight in what you've created.

## More Soap Recipes

Once you've mastered the basics of the cold-process method of soapmaking, you're ready to experiment and expand your repertoire. Using the following recipes, you'll be able to make three all-time favorites. These soap recipes use fragrance oils or essential oils and have basic additives. Use the suggested amounts of additives as a guide in making your own simple recipes.

### OATMEAL SOAP, 1-POUND RECIPE
To make this oatmeal soap you will need:

**Lye Solution**
- 6 ounces water
- 2 ounces lye

**Base Oil**
- 1 pound olive oil

## Superfat

- 1 tablespoon castor oil

## Additive

- 1 tablespoon finely ground oatmeal

## Scent Material

- 1 teaspoon combination of oatmeal, oatmeal milk, and honey fragrance oil

## Directions

1. Finely grind the oatmeal to release the skin-soothing properties for which it's so famous. If you want the look of the whole rolled-oat grain, use it sparingly since it can have sharp edges. Many soapers use baby oatmeal because it has a softer feel.

2. You can make "oat milk" by making an infusion of oatmeal and hot water. Add honey fragrance oil to the mixture.

3. Put on all protective gear, including goggles, gloves, and long sleeves.

4. Place the water in a heatproof glass 4-cup measure. Sprinkle the lye slowly and carefully into the water. Stir until dissolved. Set the lye solution aside to cool.

5. In a second heatproof glass 4-cup measure, combine the olive oil and castor oil. Warm in microwave or over boiling water. As each setup is different, be sure to watch your microwave or double boiler closely, making note of how long it takes the mixture to warm. (Don't overheat as oils take longer to cool than the lye solution does.) Set the oils aside to cool.

6. When both mixtures are at 110°F, pour the lye solution in a thin stream into the oils. Stir constantly until the mixture traces, about 10–20 minutes. If using an immersion blender, it will take about a minute. (If using an immersion blender, take care not to whip air into the mixture.)

7. Once the soap batter traces, mix in the 1 tablespoon finely ground oatmeal and 1 teaspoon of your infusion of oatmeal, oatmeal milk, and honey fragrance oil. Pour the mixture into the mold, taking care to scrape all traced soap out of the cup.

8. Cover the mold with plastic wrap, then wrap the mold in a towel for warmth and let it sit for two days.

9. Wearing your goggles and gloves, try unmolding the soap by pulling out the sides and turning the mold upside down on a brown paper bag or paper towel on your work surface. Push on the bottom of the mold. If the soap doesn't readily release, place the mold in the freezer for 1 hour. Try again to remove it. It should easily release this time.

10. Using a stainless steel knife, cut the soap log into bars. Place them on a brown paper bag to dry. Turn them daily to ensure they dry evenly.

11. Your soap will be firm and ready to use in four weeks.

## LAVENDER SOAP, 1-POUND RECIPE

Lavender essential oil has a clear to light green color and an herbal, sweetly floral smell. Here's what you'll need to make this soap:

### Lye Solution
- 6 ounces water
- 2 ounces lye

### Base Oil
- 1 pound olive oil

### Superfat
- 1 tablespoon castor oil

### Scent Material
- 1 tablespoon lavender essential oil

### Directions
1. Put on all protective gear, including goggles, gloves, and long sleeves.
2. Place the water in a heatproof glass 4-cup measure. Sprinkle the lye slowly and carefully into the water. Stir until dissolved. Set the lye solution aside to cool.
3. In a second heatproof glass 4-cup measure, combine the olive oil and castor oil. Melt in microwave or over boiling water. As each setup is different, be sure to watch your microwave or double boiler closely, making note of how long it takes the mixture to melt. (Do not overheat as oils take longer to cool than the lye solution does.) Set the oils aside to cool.
4. When both mixtures are at 110°F, pour the lye solution in a thin stream into the oils. Stir constantly until the mix-

ture traces, about 10–20 minutes. If using an immersion blender, it will take about a minute. (If using an immersion blender, take care not to whip air into the mixture.)

5. Once the soap batter traces, mix in the 1 tablespoon lavender essential oil. Pour the mixture into the mold, taking care to scrape all traced soap out of the cup.

6. Cover the mold with plastic wrap, then wrap the mold in a towel for warmth and let it sit for two days.

7. Wearing your goggles and gloves, try unmolding the soap by pulling out the sides and turning the mold upside down on a brown paper bag or paper towel on your work surface. Push on the bottom of the mold. If the soap doesn't readily release, place the mold in the freezer for 1 hour. Try again to remove it. It should easily release this time.

8. Using a stainless steel knife, cut the soap log into bars. Place them on a brown paper bag to dry. Turn them daily to ensure they dry evenly.

9. Your soap will be firm and ready to use in four weeks.

## SHEA BUTTER COMBO, 1-POUND RECIPE
This soap smells delightful and is so nourishing for the skin. Here is what you'll need:

### Lye Solution
- 6 ounces water
- 2.4 ounces lye

## Oil Blend

- 2 ounces shea butter
- 4 ounces almond oil
- 5 ounces olive oil
- 5 ounces coconut oil

## Superfat

- 1 tablespoon castor oil

## Directions

1. Put on all protective gear, including goggles, gloves, and long sleeves.

2. Place the water in a heatproof glass 4-cup measure. Sprinkle the lye slowly and carefully into the water. Stir until dissolved. Set the lye solution aside to cool.

3. In a second heatproof glass 4-cup measure, combine the shea butter, almond oil, olive oil, coconut oil, and castor oil. Melt in microwave or over boiling water. (Coconut oil has a low melting point so it will melt quickly from an opaque white solid to a clear liquid.) As each setup is different, be sure to watch your microwave or double boiler closely, making note of how long it takes the mixture to melt. (Do not overheat as oils take longer to cool than the lye solution does.) Set the oils aside to cool.

4. When both mixtures are at 110°F, pour the lye solution in a thin stream into the oils. Stir constantly until the mixture traces, about 10–20 minutes. If using an immersion blender, it will take about a minute. (If using an immersion blender, take care not to whip air into the mixture.)

5. Once the soap batter traces, pour it into the mold, taking care to scrape all traced soap out of the cup.

6. Cover the mold with plastic wrap, then wrap the mold in a towel for warmth and let it sit for two days.

7. Wearing your goggles and gloves, try unmolding the soap by pulling out the sides and turning the mold upside down on a brown paper bag or paper towel on your work surface. Push on the bottom of the mold. If the soap doesn't readily release, place the mold in the freezer for 1 hour. Try again to remove it. It should easily release this time.

8. Using a stainless steel knife, cut the soap log into bars. Place them on a brown paper bag to dry. Turn them daily to ensure they dry evenly.

9. Your soap will be firm and ready to use in four weeks.

# US/METRIC CONVERSION CHARTS

## VOLUME CONVERSIONS

| US Volume Measure | Metric Equivalent |
|---|---|
| ⅛ teaspoon | 0.5 milliliter |
| ¼ teaspoon | 1 milliliter |
| ½ teaspoon | 2 milliliters |
| 1 teaspoon | 5 milliliters |
| ½ tablespoon | 7 milliliters |
| 1 tablespoon (3 teaspoons) | 15 milliliters |
| 2 tablespoons (1 fluid ounce) | 30 milliliters |
| ¼ cup (4 tablespoons) | 60 milliliters |
| ⅓ cup | 90 milliliters |
| ½ cup (4 fluid ounces) | 125 milliliters |
| ⅔ cup | 160 milliliters |
| ¾ cup (6 fluid ounces) | 180 milliliters |
| 1 cup (16 tablespoons) | 250 milliliters |
| 1 pint (2 cups) | 500 milliliters |
| 1 quart (4 cups) | 1 liter (about) |

## WEIGHT CONVERSIONS

| US Weight Measure | Metric Equivalent |
| --- | --- |
| ½ ounce | 15 grams |
| 1 ounce | 30 grams |
| 2 ounces | 60 grams |
| 3 ounces | 85 grams |
| ¼ pound (4 ounces) | 115 grams |
| ½ pound (8 ounces) | 225 grams |
| ¾ pound (12 ounces) | 340 grams |
| 1 pound (16 ounces) | 454 grams |

## OVEN TEMPERATURE CONVERSIONS

| Degrees Fahrenheit | Degrees Celsius |
| --- | --- |
| 200 degrees F | 95 degrees C |
| 250 degrees F | 120 degrees C |
| 275 degrees F | 135 degrees C |
| 300 degrees F | 150 degrees C |
| 325 degrees F | 160 degrees C |
| 350 degrees F | 180 degrees C |
| 375 degrees F | 190 degrees C |
| 400 degrees F | 205 degrees C |
| 425 degrees F | 220 degrees C |
| 450 degrees F | 230 degrees C |

| BAKING PAN SIZES | |
| --- | --- |
| American | Metric |
| 8 x 1½ inch round baking pan | 20 x 4 cm cake tin |
| 9 x 1½ inch round baking pan | 23 x 3.5 cm cake tin |
| 11 x 7 x 1½ inch baking pan | 28 x 18 x 4 cm baking tin |
| 13 x 9 x 2 inch baking pan | 30 x 20 x 5 cm baking tin |
| 2 quart rectangular baking dish | 30 x 20 x 3 cm baking tin |
| 15 x 10 x 2 inch baking pan | 30 x 25 x 2 cm baking tin (Swiss roll tin) |
| 9 inch pie plate | 22 x 4 or 23 x 4 cm pie plate |
| 7 or 8 inch springform pan | 18 or 20 cm springform or loose bottom cake tin |
| 9 x 5 x 3 inch loaf pan | 23 x 13 x 7 cm or 2 lb narrow loaf or pate tin |
| 1½ quart casserole | 1.5 liter casserole |
| 2 quart casserole | 2 liter casserole |

# INDEX